No Rules Just Tools

Writing Tricks and Techniques for Crafting an Unputdownable Book

Julie Haase

Published by CopySitter Press
Omaha, Nebraska
All rights reserved.
Printed in the United States of America.

Not one word of this book was written using AI.

Copy Editor: Amy Handy
linkedin.com/in/amyhandy

Proofreader: Emily King
https://emilykingeditor.com

Happy stick figure graphic from Adobe Stock.
All other graphics and cover and interior design by Julie Haase.

ISBN-13: 979-8-9986036-2-4 (paperback)
ISBN-13: 979-8-9986036-3-1 (ebook)

Library of Congress Control Number: 2026908642

*to all the authors who've allowed me the privilege
of editing their books and to those who've sat
in stuffy hotel conference rooms and listened to me teach—
each experience has taught me so much and
has helped me write this book*

Contents

Introduction

I don't know about you, but I'm fascinated by words. I'm fascinated by all the ways they can be put together to create meaning—or not, depending on how well they're put together. Consider the following:

- He slunk across the room, knees bent, body folded in half, heels never touching the floor.
- He ran from the front door to the kitchen, throwing his coat onto the living room floor as he charged through.
- He pulled himself from the chair and meandered toward the hallway while he stretched, cracked his neck from side to side, and yawned.
- He jumped up from the couch and rubbed his hands together, licked his lips, and hurried to the dining room.

What do all of these sentences have in common? They all describe someone crossing a room: sneaking, rushing, heading for bed, heading to dinner. Four different purposes. Four different moods. Four different descriptions. One basic action.

That's language for you.

And I'm no expert in other languages—I speak about fifty words in French and can count to ten in Spanish and that's about it for my foreign language skills—but I don't think I'm wrong to declare that English is the most diverse language out there. Many other languages rely heavily on nonverbals—tone, inflection, volume—and context to create different meanings. In English, we just keep adding new words. *Always with the new words!*

And it fascinates me, this language of ours, that is so malleable and expandable and hard! Ask anyone who's had to learn English as a second language. English is hard!

Yet it has rules that can be followed. It has right ways and wrong ways. It has awkwardness and clarity, and the trick is to figure out how to recognize both so you can avoid the first and master the second.

And that, my friend, is why we're here. Well, it's why I'm here, and I hope it's why you're here as well—to help yourself avoid the stuff in English that hurts your use of it and to master the stuff that makes this complex language sing and makes readers of it write amazing reviews!

When I wrote the first edition of this book, I had to do a lot of research and find my footing on many of the concepts that I included in it. *Hmm, a chapter on* show, don't tell *would be good. I should probably figure out exactly what it is.* And so I did. But since then, I have been putting all that research to practical use in my own narrative writing and my editing work, and this second edition is more than just a compilation of research and some foreknowledge. Now I don't just know what *show, don't tell* is—I have really strong opinions about it!

No, really, I do. You might think that's silly. Or maybe you're thinking something along the lines of "I should hope so!" For me, it's been a journey of discovery, and I've learned more about writing and what writers can do to help themselves improve. But I've also learned about myself as both a writer and an editor. I've become stricter in some cases and more laid-back in others (although there's been much more of the former than the latter). If you've read the first edition of the book, you might notice a bit more maturity in this edition. Not to worry though; I still know how to keep it fun.

So why bother with the second edition? First of all, I've added lots of new content, including a chapter about deep POV and the "Odds and Ends" chapter, which is filled with a hodgepodge of recurring issues I encounter while editing that drive me crazy but don't warrant their own chapters (sorry, guys), so I've thrown them together. I've expanded several other chapters, including the list of commonly confused words and avoiding the BE verb. I've retooled the chapter about avoiding adverbs by adding adjectives to it in the rebranded "Writing Without Descriptors" chapter. I've also made significant edits and even some corrections in other chapters and created *all new exercises*, which is the part I'm sure you're most excited about!

Actually, let me tell you why you should be excited about that. All the information in the world will do you no good at all if you don't know how to put it to use. This is why I included exercises in the first place and why I updated them for the new edition—to help you continue to master the concepts and techniques in this book. So if you've done the exercises in the first edition, please do the new exercises too. It's like eating broccoli—it's good for you! And if you add cheese, it's really delicious! (Wait, what?)

See? I told you I'd keep it fun.

Now, before we dive in, I want to reiterate a few points from the first edition:

1. Many of the stylistic "rules" in this book do not apply to dialogue. People talk the way they talk, and you want your dialogue to be authentic. For example, there are a lot of tricks to creating great dialogue, but avoiding passive voice isn't one of them! So take the advice presented herein with a grain of salt when it comes to dialogue.

2. Don't hold me to my own rules. Remember that this book is for *narrative* writing. Prescriptive nonfiction (like how-to books, self-help books, etc.) is written very differently and

has different requirements. So, yes, I use adverbs and the BE verb, but that's because I'm literally *telling* you what to do—*showing*, apart from my many wonderful examples, would be quite inappropriate in this context.

3. Please keep in mind that some key items in this book—particularly punctuation and spelling rules—apply to American English, and not to British/UK English.

4. Where appropriate, the content of this book has been updated to align with *The Chicago Manual of Style*, 18th edition, released in September 2024. (It shouldn't surprise you to learn that taking that new book out of the box brought tears to my eyes—I know, grammar nerd!) However, the University of Chicago Press, which publishes the manual, does not endorse this book, nor should any connection between me and them be inferred in any way.

And with that out of the way, let's get you on the road to amazing narrative writing!

Part One

Adverbs, Commas, and Voice! Oh My!

Chapter 1

Avoiding the BE Verb

be, am, is, are, was, were, been, being

These words have a bad reputation in the writing world. They aren't all bad, but they tend to multiply like rabbits. If you don't stay in constant control, they will take over and drag down your writing. Learn to master these unassuming little words, and your stories will pop off the page.

Before I get into this, please note that whenever I talk about BE, I use all or small caps. This formatting is simply to distinguish the times I refer to the verb itself from the times that I actually use it *as a verb*. For example, the BE verb should not be overused. Normally, however, when talking about a word as a word, I use italics. For example, Just like BE, *feel* is often a state-of-being verb. This usage is a personal preference only. By comparison, *The Chicago Manual of Style* refers to it as the *be-verb*.

* * * * *

I've observed three interesting things about the BE verb. First, it's the single most-used verb in the English language (backed up by a kajillion websites, including Babbel's list of the twenty most common English verbs—BE is number one![1]). Second, it has the most unique forms of any English verb. Even if you lump *be*, *been*, and *being* together, you still have *am*, *is*, *are*, *was*, and *were*—that's six unique forms for one tiny verb! Finally—and this is the reason this chapter exists—it's the single most *boring* verb in the English language, as you'll see.

The Problem with BE Verbs

For such a small word, BE presents a myriad of issues when it comes to narrative writing.

BE Is a State-of-Being Verb

The class of verbs known as linking verbs exists to connect the subject of a clause to some sort of condition—or state of being—that describes the subject in one way or another. BE is the ultimate linking verb, and then there are what *Chicago* describes as "intransitive verbs that are used in a weakened sense,"[2] which include words like *become, appear, seem,* and *feel,* to name a few. These verbs might link to **what** the subject is [that building is the town hall], **who** the subject is [she's my boss], **where** the subject is [they are in Montana], or **when** the subject is [the time is nine o'clock], or they might give us a different type of condition based on the verb itself (like a feeling, an appearance, etc.).

I like to refer to linking verbs as state-of-being verbs because I'm not as interested in the verbs' grammatical purpose in the clause so much as their effect. And when it comes to those "weakened intransitive verbs,"[3] I find it easier to figure out how they're behaving in the clause if I ask myself, "Is it expressing an action or a state of being?" (versus "Is it expressing an action or linking things together?" which I don't find helpful at all). So while many authorities on the subject refer to these verbs as linking verbs, I prefer the term state-of-being verbs.

State-of-being verbs *themselves* don't tell us anything about the subject. They simply indicate the type of condition being described: physical, emotional, psychological, and so on. For example, in I feel sick, *feel* itself doesn't tell us anything about the subject. It just links the subject to the adjective, *sick,* and lets us know what type of condition we're dealing with.

But what's the big deal? Why does it matter that BE is a state-of-being verb? Well, action verbs are more interesting. As we'll continue to see throughout this chapter and beyond, action verbs are more engaging to readers and are, therefore, preferred.

* * * * *

By the way, if you're ever unsure if a verb is an action verb or a state-of-being verb, look at the words that follow it. If it's followed by a noun (I felt *lumps*) or prepositional phrase (I felt *under the cushion*), it's most likely an action verb. State-of-being verbs can be followed by nouns as well (I felt a *fool*)—but state-of-being verbs are usually separated from the noun by an article (like *a* in the above example). If the verb's followed by an adjective (I felt *tired*), it's most likely a state-of-being verb.

They looked happy.

Happy is an adjective, making *looked* a state-of-being verb.

They looked in the window.

In the window is a prepositional phrase, making *looked* an action verb.

They looked the part.

Part is a noun introduced by the article *the*. It describes their appearance, not something they were actually doing; hence, *looked* is a state-of-being verb.

BE Is Passive

State-of-being verbs are also known as passive verbs because they don't express any type of action. They have no movement. Some passive verbs—the ones that can be either active or passive—*seem* like they have movement to them. For example, the sentence I feel tired has a hint of motion to it, don't you think? There is absolutely none, but the fact that *feel* is also an action verb lends some implied movement here.

BE, on the other hand, has no movement whatsoever. It's as passive as passive can be—lifeless and . . .

BE Is Nondistinct/Nondescript

Not only is BE entirely without movement, it's also entirely without character. It's just . . . there. It could hardly be less interesting. I suppose if you used it in some sort of highly poetic way (like deliberate repetition of "I am" in a poem), you might give it some character. But in most situations, BE is simply blah.

BE Verbs Slow Your Pacing

Because of their passive nature, BE verbs do nothing to add pacing to your story. A BE here and there won't likely cause a problem, but overuse of BE verbs will definitely impact the pacing. And if you're writing a story or scene that needs to feel urgent, suspenseful, scary, exciting, or even just happy, the BE verb can really work against you.

BE Verbs Negatively Impact Reader Engagement

All this adds up to low reader engagement, especially if BE shows up over and over and over again in one form or another. Later we're going to talk about how to improve word choices to increase reader engagement. Step one is to minimize use of the BE verb.

When to Replace It

Whenever possible! You'll never be wrong in the decision to replace BE with a better verb. So the question isn't really *when* you should try to replace it but rather *how* to replace it. That's a much trickier question to answer.

As you encounter BE verbs in your story, ask yourself the following three questions, one at a time, until you find the answer that works.

Question One: Can it be replaced with an action verb?

Sometimes it really is as simple as just replacing one verb with another, preferably putting in an action verb. This doesn't always work, but when it does, it's like wordsmithing magic!

The dogs **are** outside.
The dogs **went** outside.

This is a simple swap-in of an action verb. Sure, it's not a very exciting action verb, but *went* has something that *are* will never have—movement. And that's all it takes. It's an immediate improvement in reader engagement, regardless of how small that improvement may seem.

Question Two: Is a rewrite more appropriate?

Perhaps swapping the BE verb for an action verb isn't working because you can't find an appropriate action verb or you just don't like what you've come up with. That's OK. The next step is to consider a rewrite.

Now don't panic. I'm not suggesting you retool an entire paragraph to get rid of one BE verb. Linguistic acrobatics are not necessary here. Ideally, you want to tweak or possibly rewrite just the sentence the BE verb appears in. (Of course, if you want to retool the entire paragraph, go for it. You might wind up with a much better paragraph just to replace one little word—it can happen!)

The dogs are outside.
I let the dogs out when I got home.

Question Three: Can it be replaced with another state-of-being verb?

If using an action verb or trying a rewrite isn't working, then perhaps just using a better state-of-being verb is the answer. As I mentioned before, some passive verbs seem like they have movement to them even though they don't. If you're stuck using a state-of-being verb, one of these other verbs is definitely a step up from the BE verb. Sure, it's still a passive verb, but at least it seems more interesting than that.

They **are** excited.
They **look** excited.

(They're not looking around excitedly. We're talking about their appearance, a.k.a. their *state of being*. It kind of sounds like an action though, doesn't it? Mic drop.)

What if all three answers are NO?
Leave the BE verb as is! That's right. At the end of the day, you do not need to remove every single BE verb every single time. As I said before, this is an essential word. You will *never* avoid it entirely, nor should you try. Sometimes it's actually the appropriate verb to use (keep reading), and sometimes it's just the only verb that works. So don't kill yourself trying to get rid of it. Replace or remove the occurrences that you can, and let the others *be* (wink, wink).

When Not to Replace It

Leaving in BE verbs isn't just an "I don't know what else to do with it" last resort. There are, in fact, times when the BE verb is appropriate or even necessary.

Subdued Pacing and Mood
When you're going for slower pacing or a laid-back tone, the BE verb can help. You still don't want to overdo it, simply because it

can get too repetitive, but feel free to pepper in BE verbs to support the vibe you're trying to establish. No verb in the English language is more subdued than BE!

Creating Progressive Tense

BE is often used as an auxiliary verb to help create the verb tense known as the progressive. This is one of those times when BE's essential nature comes into play because you simply cannot create progressive tense without it. In these circumstances, the question to ask is not whether the BE verb can be replaced but whether use of the progressive tense is appropriate.

So first of all, what the heck is progressive tense? It's a form that expresses an ongoing action through the use of a present participle.

OK, wait, this is getting weirdly technical. Hang in there with me. We'll get through it together!

When you slap an -ing ending onto a verb, you create a present participle. Now, there are words that end in -ing that are not present participles: *sting, nothing, wing*. But if you take an otherwise unsuspecting verb and add -ing to the end (*flying, watching, stinging*), you create a present participle. Don't freak out here but . . . there are no exceptions! Verb + ING = Present Participle. Every time!

Present participles can act as verbs, nouns (a.k.a. gerunds), and adjectives. When they act as verbs, they are combined with a BE verb and, voilà!, progressive tense.

Present Progressive: She is going.

Past Progressive: She was going.

Future Progressive: She will be going.

Present Perfect Progressive: She has been going.

Past Perfect Progressive: She had been going.

Future Perfect Progressive: She will have been going.

Phew! Who can remember all of that?! Don't worry—you don't have to. All you need to remember is that sometimes we use the progressive tense unnecessarily. Consider the following examples:

> They were making sandwiches. = They made sandwiches.
> She is making sandwiches. = She makes sandwiches.
> She will be making sandwiches. = She will make sandwiches.

Now I'm hungry. But do you notice what I did there? I changed the past, present, and future *progressive* tenses into *simple* past, present, and future tenses. Sometimes we use the progressive tense when it's really not appropriate. Consider this example:

> He was going to the store while I was practicing yoga.

Two ongoing actions. Is that necessary if both actions are already completed? Probably not.

> He went to the store while I was practicing yoga.

This version means that the first action was completed during the second action. This is one of the most appropriate uses of progressive tense—something was taking place when something else happened (one ongoing action, one completed action).

> He went to the store while I practiced yoga.

Here we mean that both actions are complete and it doesn't really matter that one took place at the same time as the other (though *while* does make this clear). They're both simply done.

The progressive tense is very appropriate—at times. So when you encounter **BE + Present Participle**, ask yourself if you can change to simple past, present, or future without marring the meaning. If so, then you probably should. If not, then keep the progressive tense as is.

(By the way, there's more on this topic in chapter 8.)

Creating Subjunctive Mood

To borrow a definition from *A Writer's Reference*, 9th edition, the subjunctive mood expresses "wishes, requests, or conditions contrary to fact."[4]

> I wish I were taller.
> If he were here, he'd know what to do.

The subjunctive is sometimes considered a tense, but it's not one. It's a mood, along with the imperative (telling people what to do) and the indicative (everything else).

Subjunctive mood cannot be created with any other verb, and it's traditionally created using *were*; however, use of *was* is becoming more acceptable as a less formal alternative (I wish I was taller). *Was* sounds weird to me in this construction, but it's definitely appropriate, especially in dialogue.

As a general rule, a third-person narrator is probably more likely to use *were*, while first-person narrators and other characters will use *were* or *was* depending on the type of character they are (how they were raised, where they're from, how much/what type of education they've had, how snooty they are, etc.).

But the one thing that is certain is that they will use a BE verb because you can't make the subjunctive without it.

Telling Something Outright

We'll get into the mechanics of "telling" in the *show, don't tell* chapter. For now, just keep in mind that the BE verb tells—it states things outright, no beating about the bush, no softening the blow, no [insert alternate cliché here—until we get to chapter 12!].

> She was first in her class.
> He is an engineer.
> They are not sure what to do.

Sometimes a simple statement of fact is just what you need to impart necessary information to readers, and as we'll discuss later, that's absolutely valid. And no word tells as plainly as the BE verb, so when it's appropriate, tell away.

It, There, That, This/These

It, there, that, and *this/these* are acceptable, albeit uninteresting, pronouns that are often combined with BE as the subject/verb of a clause (for example, It was raining outside or That is not acceptable). Try not to overdo these nondescript combos, because they are the ultimate in mundane writing (boring pronoun + boring verb = not a great way to start a sentence if you want readers to be interested). And the good news is that you will almost always be able to find another way to say it (for example, for this sentence, I started to write, "*there is* almost always another way to say it"—obviously, I was right). Use these combos, just not too much.

> There were a lot of clouds in the sky. = Clouds filled the sky.
> It was cold outside. − The temperature hovered around zero degrees.
> This is a bad idea. = This idea stinks.

Note that, in the third example, I'm still using *this,* but as an adjective, not a pronoun. *This, these,* and *that* can often be ambiguous as pronouns (This stinks—this what?). In many cases, it's necessary to use them with the noun they refer to instead of using them on their own (*This idea* stinks).

Review and Replace

Previously I said to review your copy closely and decide if each BE verb can be replaced. That can be a very daunting task, especially if you've never given this little verb much thought before and are therefore facing the possibility of hundreds of occurrences, if not thousands, in a single manuscript. Ouch. The first thing you need to do here is to settle in and get comfortable with the idea that it's going to take a decent chunk of time to find and deal with all those verbs.

Here's one method for dealing with what could be an abundance of BE verbs. You might want to practice this method on a short story or a single chapter before you try to tackle an entire book.

NOTE: Don't do any of this until you're on an almost final draft! It would be a huge waste of time to do all of this on an early draft that's likely to change significantly before you're done.

1. Start with Find/Replace. This is handy for a simple swap-out of verbs (replacing BE with action or better state-of-being verbs). Do a separate find for each form of the verb (*am, is, are, was, were*). For each occurrence, determine if you can replace it with an action verb. If you find a replacement action verb, replace the BE verb and move on to the next occurrence. Take your time and really give each occurrence some careful thought. It's a tedious exercise, but you'll be amazed at what you'll learn if you take it seriously and slowly. Over time, you'll probably notice your first-draft writing improving as

you train yourself to recognize BE verbs and avoid them up front.

2. As you're going through the Find/Replace exercise, label any BE verbs you don't change by highlighting them in different colors (seriously, you're going to learn a lot from this and get better at writing without BE verbs, so don't scoff). Label the following using a different color for each:
   - BE verbs you can't simply replace with an action verb
   - BE verbs being used as auxiliary (or "helping") verbs (i.e., in conjunction with another verb), like is waiting, were thrown, was masked
   - *Were/Was* being used in the subjunctive mood

3. Once you're done with the Find/Replace for each form of the verb, go through the manuscript and look for all the BE verbs you couldn't replace and determine if a rewrite would work. If so, go for it. If not, decide if a better state-of-being verb would work. If neither of these options pans out, just remove the highlight and move on (i.e., leave the verb as is).

4. Go through again and look at all the auxiliary BE verbs. Are you using passive voice (see chapter 3)? Is it an unnecessary use of the progressive tense? Fix the ones that need it, and remove the highlight from any you determine to be appropriate.

5. After all this, you should just have your subjunctive occurrences of *were* and *was* still highlighted. Double-check them just to make sure you feel good about your use of the subjunctive. Adjust any of them as necessary. Remove the highlight from the rest.

Success! Yes, you've just spent an annoying amount of time dealing with a single verb, but you've gotten a lot of practice at replacing it, which will eventually parlay into experience for avoiding it in the first place.

And speaking of avoiding, let's talk about that for a hot second. The more often you stop yourself from using the BE verb as you write, the more often you'll *be able to stop* yourself (i.e., you'll get better and better at avoiding it). For example, let's say you're writing along and start typing "She was hungry for" and then you realize you've written *was*. So you stop, you consider for a moment, then you change it to "She hungered for" and move on. Eventually, you'll get good at recognizing when you should or should not use it as you go, which will mean fewer stops as you write and fewer replacements during revisions.

Finally, those tedious steps I just outlined will also help you learn to recognize when a BE verb is being used as an auxiliary verb, which will also help you recognize when you're using passive voice (again, see chapter 3) and when you might be overusing the progressive tense, both of which require a BE auxiliary verb.

For example:

Progressive Tense:
He *was running* the shop last summer. = He *ran* the shop last summer.

Passive Voice:
The shop *was run* all summer long. = He *ran* the shop all summer long.

TO BE or Not TO BE?
(I don't know. I can't help myself!)

See the examples below. Would you replace the BE verbs in these sentences or leave them as is? If you think they should be replaced, go ahead and give it a whirl. See my answers on page 216.

1. Clair *was* tired so she turned in early.

2. The banners *were* hung around the town square for the celebration.

3. *Are* you going to the show with Jessica?

4. There *are* too many books to fit on this shelf.

5. Lin *is* always trying to outdo his brother.

6. I'*m* not a fan of horror movies.

7.   How did you know she *was* lying?

8.   Carmine *is* the biggest goofball I've ever met.

9.   The wind *is* really howling tonight.

10.   That *was* the best meal I've ever eaten.

Extra Challenge!

Write for ten minutes without using a single BE verb. Write whatever you want or, if you can't think of a topic, here's a prompt: A dinghy floats empty in the middle of a lake. How did it get there? (I dare you to make it funny!) Time yourself and check your work when you're done. Did you avoid BE verbs? If not, try to replace any that you used. Good luck!

Chapter 2

Writing Without Descriptors

Descriptors refers to words that describe, or modify, other words. Descriptors are also known as adjectives and adverbs. You'll probably never write entirely without them, but minimizing their usage will help you create stronger, more engaging stories.

OK, I know that the idea of writing without a single adjective or adverb is beyond a head-scratcher. Maybe adverbs, but adjectives? The whole idea seems a bit unreasonable, doesn't it? Or maybe it sounds terrifying or unbelievably daunting to you. Don't freak out. It can be done, and *you can do it*. And when you get to the *show, don't tell* chapter, you'll understand even more how writing without descriptors can make your story better.

But to say that descriptors should be avoided at all costs would be hyperbole. Whether adjectives or adverbs, descriptors serve a purpose, just like any other part of speech. In narrative writing, however, they can detract from the overall quality and reduce reader engagement and enjoyment. So don't ever feel compelled to get rid of them completely, but I do recommend that you learn how to avoid them and do so at every logical opportunity.

Descriptors Defined

So that I'm not making any assumptions about your understanding of these terms, let's spend a minute defining them.

Adjectives

Adjectives modify nouns, and there are many types of adjectives, most of which are so irrelevant to our discussion that I'm not going to bother to list them. We're concerned about *descriptive* adjectives only—red, noisy, jealous, insightful, tall, smelly, and so on.

Adverbs

An adverb is a modifier used to describe or intensify verbs, adjectives, and other adverbs.

Most adverbs end in -ly, but not all of them, and not every word that ends in -ly is an adverb.

She cried *softly*.
Softly is an adverb modifying *cried*.

She cried *again*.
Again is also an adverb modifying *cried*.

He took the *only* donut.
Only is an adjective modifying *donut*.
Only can also be used as an adverb, just in case you weren't already confused!

Are Descriptors Evil?

Mark Twain (presumably) said, "Adverbs are the tool of the lazy writer." The same thing could be said (although perhaps to a lesser degree) about adjectives. But are they *evil*? Are they out to destroy your writing and expose you as a charlatan who can't survive without the words *really* and *simple* and *suddenly*?

No, of course not. Descriptors have their place (and you're not a charlatan). But before you can learn to use them effectively, you need to understand what makes them problematic.

Descriptors *tell*.
Speaking of *show, don't tell*, descriptors tell, as in, they spell out exactly what you want the reader to know without invoking the reader's imagination. Through proper setting of a scene and use of strong nouns and verbs, a surprisingly high percentage of descriptors can be eliminated.

Consider this sentence:

He closed the door loudly.

What does closing a door loudly look like? The adverb gives you information but it doesn't exactly paint a picture.

The wall shook when he slammed the door, and the sound reverberated down the hallway.

Do you find this sentence more impactful? It doesn't feature a single adjective or adverb.

How about the following sentence?

Blowing snow made it difficult to see while driving.

Not only do we have two adjectives (*blowing* and *difficult*) but we also have an ambiguous *it* that exists just to allow us to use the word *difficult*.

The snow swirled in the wind, blinding my headlights in their search for the road.

The adjectives have been removed and replaced with more interesting nouns and verbs to create a more engaging description—without any descriptors!

Descriptors put lipstick on a pig.
In other words, descriptors often do little more than dress up weak nouns and verbs. Use strong nouns and verbs and you won't need to gussy them up with unnecessary modifiers.

Reference the door-closing example. *Closed* is a weak verb and *loudly* does little to make it better. Changing the verb to *slammed* removes any need for an adverb and paints a much clearer picture of the scene.

Descriptors can cause wordiness.

By wordiness, I mean the use of unnecessary or redundant words, not an excessive number of words. Why say worked quickly when you can say hustled? Why say towering building when you can say skyscraper (or tower!)? Not only will you cut down on wordiness, but you'll have stronger, more descriptive words to build with.

On the subject of word count, you may find that the best way to replace a single, ineffective descriptor is to use a much longer description.

Consider our previous example:

Blowing snow made it difficult to see while driving.
The snow swirled in the wind, blinding my headlights in their search
   for the road.

Sure, the second sentence is longer than the first one, but it's also much more interesting. You want to be concise in your writing, but a good *description* outweighs a boring *descriptor* any day of the week.

Descriptors can be redundant.

We have a tendency to embellish words with descriptors that mean the same, or almost the same, as the words they're modifying: run quickly, give generously, brave hero, deadly bullet, and so on. These descriptors add very little to the narrative. They aren't actually descriptive—or interesting. All they do is take up space.

Now, you may be thinking that these descriptors add intensity to the words they modify, and in some cases you may be right. However, there are much better ways to accomplish that.

For example, *running* means to move fast, so what does *quickly* tell us? Nothing. Because it means roughly the same thing as the verb, the adverb doesn't add anything. Instead of using a bland adverb, try using a more descriptive verb. Or describe the action in more visceral terms. Describe what the action looked and felt like and bring the reader into the moment.

Boring: He ran quickly toward the fire.

Better: He sped toward the fire.

Yes!: Adrenaline, like rocket fuel pumping through his veins, hurtled him toward the flames.

Note that not only have we removed the adverb but we've given a pretty great description without adjectives as well.

Descriptors can sound repetitive.

When it comes to adverbs, most of which end in -ly, that "lee" ending can start to sound repetitive, even singsongy. This repetitiveness can interrupt the flow and the mood of your writing and can pull readers out of the story.

She quickly crossed the street, as the wind mercilessly swirled around her, constantly flicking her brightly colored skirt into the air. She nervously tried to hold the fabric down, but the gusts repeatedly tore the skirt from her hands.

You could write this instead:

She raced across the street as the wind whipped around her, grabbing and flicking her skirt into the air. She tried to hold the fabric down, but no matter what she did, the wind tore the skirt from her hands. (*Zero descriptors!*)

When it comes to adjectives, the problem occurs when we use too many of them in a row: the tall, dark, handsome, mysterious hooded man. All right already! Draw out the description and find other ways to impart these details (assuming that all of them are even necessary):

> The man stood in the shadows, a lock of hair poking out from his hood. *Hmm, Johnny Depp, only taller,* Avery thought as she stared at his eyes glistening in the half dark. *Who is he? What does he want?*

Here I've sprinkled in the description instead of just listing a bunch of features. Also, I've done something that we'll talk about more later—I've used the character's thoughts to help share information. And yes, this rewrite is longer, but I hope we can agree that it's both more descriptive and more interesting.

Tips for Dealing with Descriptors

Look for those -ly endings.

Since most adverbs end in -ly, a search for that word ending will locate the majority of your adverbs. As you review them, ask yourself if the adverb is enhancing the writing, if it could be removed without changing the meaning, or if you can get rid of it by using a stronger verb (or whatever word the adverb is modifying). Would you rather use the light came on intermittently or the light flickered? Do you need to say she suddenly jumped out, or can you just say she jumped out (an action that implies a certain level of suddenness on its own)?

Look out for intensifiers.

One type of adverb is known as an intensifier: *really, very, so.* Intensifiers, well, *intensify* other descriptors, and they often mask weak descriptors (he was really mad versus he was enraged). As you look for opportunities to limit descriptor use, you will automatically reduce use of intensifiers as well. But for those descriptors you keep, be sure they're good ones, preferably ones that do not need to be intensified.

Be aware of noun adjectives.

Nouns often act as adjectives (*fairy* godmother, *tree* trimmer, *bank* teller), and most of the time, the second noun in the phrase would not make sense or would not be clear enough without the noun adjective (there is a massive difference between a godmother and a *fairy* godmother). Besides, as I said earlier, we're concerned about descriptive adjectives only, and noun adjectives don't necessarily fall into that category. So leave noun adjectives be.

Look for state-of-being verbs.

State-of-being verbs—like *be, feel,* and *become*—are often followed by adjectives (I am happy, I feel happy, I became happy), so keeping an eye out for these types of verbs can help you identify adjectives as well. Often, state-of-being verbs present us with great *show, don't tell* moments in which descriptions of the subject's *actions* are more engaging to readers and eliminate the need for somewhat stale state-of-being verbs and adjectives. Learn more in chapter 9.

Judge the nouns and verbs first.

As you find adverbs and adjectives in your writing and you're trying to decide if they're necessary, don't just evaluate the descriptors themselves. Evaluate the nouns and verbs they're modifying. In a sentence like The painting was ugly, is *ugly* the problem or is *was* the problem? If we used a better verb, would the adjective even be necessary?

Descriptors Are Not the Enemy

Adjectives in particular can be very difficult to get rid of because sometimes they're actually essential. Additionally, sometimes you just need to state something outright and move on (again, see the *show, don't tell* chapter), and descriptors help you do that. Finally, sometimes there just isn't any better or more appropriate way to say something (such as when trying to maintain a narrator's or character's voice).

That said, adverbs should be used only when they truly contribute to the text. Go through your writing and flag all the adverbs. Spend some time with each one and decide if you can replace them with something better (or simply remove them). Sparse, effective use of adverbs will make your writing much stronger and more interesting to read.

The Bottom Line About Descriptors

The main issue with adjectives and adverbs is that they *tell*, meaning they don't give readers the opportunity to use their imaginations, to discover the story details on their own, and to be fully immersed in the experience. However, as you'll learn, telling is not all bad and must be used from time to time to balance out all the showing. So the bottom line? *Practice show, don't tell!* You'll naturally wind up limiting your descriptors, and your writing will get better and better over time.

Practice Replacing Descriptors

Try to rewrite the following sentences without using the descriptors. (Don't just delete the descriptors. Revise the sentences to make the descriptors obsolete. Be creative.) See my answers on page 218.

1. I expected the used car salesman to be *slimy* and *creepy* and a *big fat* liar, but he was *actually really great.*

2. The *rolling* hills stretched out with their *tall waving* grasses in the *warm* sunshine.

3. His new car gleamed *brightly* in *strikingly crisp metallic* black.

4. She bought a variety of *silly* toys and *goofy* prizes for the party.

5. The drive was *boring* and I *nearly* feel asleep at the wheel.

6. I'd rather eat *crisp, juicy* cucumber slices than put them on my *puffy* eyes.

7. "Wanna get a drink?" she said as she smiled *openly* and *accidentally* revealed an *unknown* hunk of spinach stuck between her *otherwise perfect* teeth.

8. The *giant brown-and-white* dog lay on the *sun-kissed* patio and napped *peacefully*.

9. He set the *beautiful and ornate* table using his grandparents' *vintage* china.

10. "Grab that *big* book off the top shelf. No, the *red* one. The *big red* one!"

Chapter 3

Passive Voice Explained

When you're writing a story, you want your words to carry your readers forward in an engaging and, often, exciting way. Passive voice can be counter to this goal, so learning to avoid it as much as possible is a must for every narrative writer.

What Is Voice?

In grammar, voice refers to who in the sentence is performing the action of the verb—the subject of the sentence or someone or something else. (This should not be confused with *the author's, the narrator's, or a character's voice*, which is an entirely different type of voice and not discussed in this book.)

There are two voices: active and passive.

In active voice, the subject of the sentence performs the action of the verb: Timmy threw the ball.

In passive voice, the subject of the sentence is being acted upon, and the action of the verb is being performed by someone or something else: The ball was thrown by Timmy.

Another way to say it is that the object of the verb becomes the subject of the sentence. *Ball* is the object of the verb but has been placed in the subject position.

object → subject
↓   ↓
Timmy threw the ball.   The ball was thrown by Timmy.

Other examples:

Active: The rancher herds the cattle.
Passive: The cattle are herded by the rancher.
In both examples, the rancher is performing the action of herding.

Active: The setting sun illuminated the low-hanging clouds.
Passive: The low-hanging clouds were illuminated by the setting sun.
In both examples, the sun is doing the illuminating.

When Does a Sentence Have a Voice?

Not all sentences are in active or passive voice. Voice only exists when using what are called transitive verbs, which are verbs that require an object in order to make sense. The object answers the question *what?* or *who?* of the verb.

For example: They brought a bottle of red wine.

If I just said they brought, it wouldn't make sense. You would be left wondering, brought what? The object *bottle [of red wine]* answers that question, proving that *brought* is a transitive verb and making this sentence active voice.

Intransitive verbs do not require an object: They waited for hours.

Can you ask, *waited what?* or *waited who?* No. In fact, those questions make no sense at all. That's because *wait* is an intransitive verb. (To be clear, you can ask, *waited **for** what?* But the verb isn't *wait for*. It's *wait*. If you have to add a preposition after the verb to be able to ask *what?* or *who?* then you're dealing with an intransitive verb.) Consequently, this sentence has no voice (poor thing).

They brought a bottle of red wine. = Active Voice
The wine was brought by them. = Passive Voice
They waited for hours. = No voice.

OK, you don't have to understand or remember all that transitive/intransitive stuff. I just want you to understand that not all sentences have voice.

Why Does Voice Matter?

As the name suggests, active voice is engaging to readers. It's more present and immediate than passive voice. In most writing, fiction and nonfiction alike, active voice is preferred because it's better at moving a narrative forward and keeping the reader's attention.

Active voice is also an absolute must for suspenseful, exciting, and all-around fast-paced scenes. Passive voice will only slow down the story and decrease the tension.

Is Passive Voice Always Wrong?

Absolutely not. Sometimes passive voice is exactly what the narrative calls for. If the tone is subdued, melancholy, or otherwise low-key or if the story is meant to move forward slowly, then passive voice can help create the right mood and pace.

Another reason to use passive voice is to leave out or disguise who is performing the action. This is called an unnamed performer. For example, we may not need to know that Timmy threw the ball, or we may want to hide from the reader the fact that Timmy threw it. That would be impossible in active voice, so in those cases, passive voice is required. We'll discuss the unnamed performer more in a bit.

Finally, sometimes changing a sentence to active voice requires linguistic acrobatics that are both complicated to write and confusing to read. In these situations, keeping the sentence passive is the better choice.

Recognizing Passive Voice

The quickest way to identify passive voice is to figure out who is performing the action of the verb, as described previously. If you can do this, you're golden.

However, that's not always clear, and you may benefit from

understanding the grammatical construction of passive voice. First, let's define some terms.

Auxiliary Verb

As described in chapter 1, auxiliary verbs are used in combination with another verb to form different voices and tenses. A few of the auxiliary verbs are *be, have, can, do,* and *may.*

Examples:

<table>
<tr><td>He was leaving.</td><td>She may continue.</td></tr>
<tr><td>They had chosen.</td><td>You did forget.</td></tr>
<tr><td>They can remember.</td><td>I am running.</td></tr>
</table>

Each example has two verbs: the auxiliary verb (in italics) and the principal verb (*leaving, chosen, remember, continue, forget, running*).

Participles

Basically, a participle is a verb that acts as an adjective. Participles can also be combined with auxiliary verbs to form certain tenses and voices. There are two types of participles.

Present Participles, which we looked at in chapter 1, show a continuing action and *always* end in -ing. *All verbs ending in the suffix -ing* are present participles (*tying, coping,* and *looking* are present participles; *bring, sting,* and *cling* are not).

Past Participles show a completed action, and most end in -ed.

<table>
<tr><td>Present Participle Examples:</td><td>Past Participle Examples:</td></tr>
<tr><td>running water</td><td>fallen angel</td></tr>
<tr><td>giving tree</td><td>grilled chicken</td></tr>
<tr><td>rolling hills</td><td>masked man</td></tr>
</table>

Constructing Passive Voice

Now, when you're looking for passive voice, you're looking for two things: an auxiliary BE verb and a *past* participle. Let's look at our earlier examples:

$$\text{auxiliary BE verb} \qquad \text{past participle}$$
$$\downarrow \qquad\qquad \downarrow$$

The ball was thrown by Timmy.

$$\text{auxiliary BE verb} \qquad \text{past participle}$$
$$\downarrow \qquad\qquad \downarrow$$

The cattle are herded by the rancher.

$$\text{auxiliary BE verb} \qquad \text{past participle}$$
$$\downarrow \qquad\qquad \downarrow$$

The low-hanging clouds were illuminated by the setting sun.

Tips for Recognizing Passive Voice

Figure Out Who Is Performing the Action of the Verb

Find your verb and figure out who is doing (or experiencing) whatever the verb describes.

Except in cases of inverted sentences, if the performer appears in the sentence *before* the verb, you're in active voice. If the performer appears *after* the verb, you're most likely in passive voice.

Consider our previous examples:

Active: Timmy threw the ball.
Passive: The ball was thrown by Timmy.

Timmy is performing the action of the verb in both sentences. In the active sentence, he appears before the verb. In the passive sentence, he appears after the verb.

But what if we had said this: The ball was thrown hard.

We've left poor little Timmy out of this sentence completely. That's an example of the unnamed performer, which occurs fairly often in passive voice. Maybe we already know who's throwing the ball, or maybe it doesn't matter who's doing it. Or maybe you don't *want* the reader to know who threw the ball.

It doesn't matter why the performer was left out. All that matters right now is that our best and easiest way to identify passive voice has been stolen from us. *Not cool.* However, note that an unnamed performer never exists in active voice (unless you count the understood *you*, as in "[you] Take out the trash," but here we've removed the subject of the sentence, not just the performer of the verb). If you have a subject and a verb, but the performer of the action is unnamed, you are in passive voice.

There is a trick to test this. I call it the "by so-and-so" trick. In the ball was thrown by Timmy, Timmy is our so-and-so; therefore, we have the info we need. In the ball was thrown hard, we have no "by so-and-so" to guide us. The trick, then, is to add our own "by so-and-so" after the verb.

The ball was thrown [by so-and-so] hard.

We can do that with passive voice but not with active voice:

Timmy threw [by so-and-so] the ball.

Not only do we already know that Timmy threw the ball, so why would we even try this, but also it doesn't make any dang sense. The second sentence is definitely active voice.

Check for a BE Verb

Does your sentence use *am, is, are, was,* or *were?* If it doesn't, then you are not in passive voice. If it does, then you have one-half of a passive voice verb. Now check for the other half.

Does the Sentence Have a Past Participle?

Your BE verb must be combined with a *past* participle in order to create passive voice.

If BE is the only verb, the sentence is not in passive voice. If the principal verb ends in the suffix -ing, you have a present participle and the sentence is, therefore, not in passive voice.

A BE verb all by itself is not enough to create passive voice.
↓
He is the king.

An auxiliary BE verb could   But this is a present participle,
mean passive voice.   so it's active voice.
↓   ↓
He is becoming the king.

Auxiliary BE verb + past participle = passive voice.
↓   ↓
He was crowned the king.

Compound and Complex Sentences

So here's a wrinkle. You can have both active voice and passive voice in the same sentence. It hardly seems fair, but it's true. And sometimes that's OK.

A couple of quick definitions before we start:

An **independent clause** has a subject and verb and contains a complete thought (i.e., it can stand on its own): I bought a new dress.

A **dependent clause** has a subject and verb plus a subordinating conjunction, like *because, since, that, when, as, before,* and *if.* A dependent clause does not contain a complete thought. It cannot stand **on its own:** when I bought a new dress.

Compound Sentences

A compound sentence is one in which two (or more) independent clauses are combined by a coordinating conjunction (*and, or, but,* etc.). Try to keep both clauses in active voice. For example:

Original Sentence:
He honked the horn, but his efforts were ignored.
(His efforts were ignored **is passive.**)

Change to:
He honked the horn, but the goats ignored his efforts.
(He honked the horn **and** the goats ignored his efforts **are both** active.)

Complex Sentences

A complex sentence is made up of one independent clause and at least one dependent clause.

Her feet hurt because she stood in line for four hours.

Only the independent clause (the one without the conjunction) needs to be in active voice. Well, let me qualify that statement. *In my opinion,* only the independent clause needs to be in active voice. Other sources will tell you otherwise, but obviously I'm your friend and they are evil.

OK, that's not fair. Let's split the difference. The *preference* is to have both clauses in active voice, but if you can't make that work for whatever reason, I give you permission to make the dependent clause passive.

He honked the horn, although his efforts were ignored.

Here we've changed our previous example from a compound

sentence using the coordinating conjunction *but* to a complex sentence using the subordinating conjunction *although*. It may seem silly to say that such a simple change means we no longer need to use active voice in the second clause, which is why the preference is to keep both clauses active.

Let me put some context to my opinion. Dependent clauses are cling-ons. They're along for the ride and can't stand on their own. Therefore, the independent clause carries the weight of the sentence. So as long as that clause is in active voice, you're going to maintain your pacing. Of course, you don't want all of your dependent clauses to be passive—everything in moderation, right? But the occasional passive dependent clause never hurt anybody.

Compound-Complex Sentences

A compound-complex sentence is a complex sentence with two or more independent clauses combined by a coordinating conjunction. Each of the independent clauses should be in active voice.

> He honked the horn, although his efforts were ignored, and he waited for twenty minutes for the goats to cross the road.
>
> (He honked the horn **and** he waited for twenty minutes for the goats to cross the road **are independent clauses in active voice.**)

Passive Voice Versus Active Voice

Can you tell which of the following sentences are passive voice and which are active voice?

1. Luna was hoping for a miracle, but the package didn't arrive on time.
2. Given the circumstances, he felt compelled to pitch in with the cleanup.
3. How many people were chosen to receive prizes?
4. It's comical that you think I believe anything you say!
5. Sunlight poked through but was mostly obscured by the clouds.
6. Are the Smiths coming to the party?
7. Under no circumstances would I cheat on a test.
8. I can't remember if Nathan was driven home or if he drove himself.
9. After leaving work, Jasmine was tired and decided to pick up dinner on her way home.
10. The baker was relieved that his flour was delivered on time.

Answers:

1. **Active Voice:** "Was hoping" may seem passive because of that BE verb, but *hoping* is a present participle and passive voice requires a past participle. In the second clause, *didn't arrive* is also active voice.
2. **Active Voice:** Although *felt* is a passive state-of-being verb, this sentence is in simple past tense with no BE verb. Plus, *compelled* is an adjective in this sentence, not a verb.

3. **Passive Voice:** Questions can be tricky, but notice that this sentence has both a BE verb (*were*) and a past participle (*chosen*). Also notice that we have an unnamed performer of the action (Who made the choice? We don't know!).

4. **Active Voice:** Although the *is* in *it's* is a BE verb, there is no past participle. Additionally, *you think, I believe,* and *you say* are all active voice.

5. **Both Voices:** This sentence features a compound verb: *poked* and *was obscured. Poked* is active voice, but *was obscured* is passive. Notice the BE verb (*was*), the past participle (*obscured*), and the "by so-and-so" phrase (*by the clouds*).

6. **Active Voice:** We have a BE verb right out of the gate (*are*), but we follow it up with a present participle (*coming*).

7. **Active Voice:** Inverted sentences like this one can be tough to figure out, but find the verb(s) and, if necessary, put together multi-word verbs that have been split up. In this sentence, the verb is *would cheat.* No BE verb. No past participle.

8. **Both Voices:** The independent clause uses active voice (*can['t] remember*), but the first dependent clause uses passive voice (*was driven*). The second dependent clause is active (*drove*).

9. **Active Voice:** Although *tired* looks like a past participle—it ends in -ed, after all—it's actually an adjective in this sentence, not a verb. Here are a few tests you can try when you aren't sure if a past participle is acting as a verb or an adjective in a sentence: (1) Try adding *very* in front of the participle. *Very* is an intensifier that modifies adjectives and adverbs, not verbs, so if adding it makes sense (Jasmine was very tired), then your participle is probably an adjective. (2) Try adding a "by so-and-so" phrase. If you can't do so without changing the meaning of the sentence, then your participle is probably not a verb. (3)

Try rearranging the sentence. If you can't—I don't know any way to rearrange Jasmine was tired without adding new details and changing the meaning of the sentence (or sounding like Yoda)—then your participle is most likely an adjective.

10. **Both Voices:** See what I did here? The first clause (the baker was relieved) is active voice because, just like *tired* in #9, *relieved* is an adjective. But the second clause (that his flour was delivered on time) is passive voice because *delivered* is a verb.

Changing Passive to Active

Try changing the following passive sentences to active. Build on what you've learned! Can you also remove any descriptors and BE verbs? See my answers on page 221.

Remember, in order for a sentence to be in active voice, the performer of the action must be the subject. Therefore, you first need to figure out who or what is performing the action of the passive verb.

Also keep in mind that in a complex sentence (see definition on page 43), only the independent clause needs to be in active voice; however, it's good practice to try making all clauses active, so go for it.

1. Why *were* Christians *thrown* to the lions in ancient Rome?

2. Everyone *was captivated* by the speaker.

3. The logo *was reimagined* by the new designer.

4. The puppy *was inoculated* before it *was brought* home.

5. Susan *was forced* to testify by court order, but she pled the Fifth.

6. Everyone thought the *Titanic was built* to withstand anything.

7. Banks in the Old West *were* often *robbed.*

8. He *was presumed* guilty of cheating because he'd never gotten an A on a test before.

9. People on both sides of the issue *were stunned* by the vicious attack.

10. I don't see how she *was fooled* by such an obvious lie.

Chapter 4

Grammar Errors? Maybe Not

Regardless of what your high school grammar textbook said, not all the so-called errors we've learned about are bad. Some aren't even considered errors anymore. And others, while still technically "wrong," can be used to add impact to your writing.

Not everyone agrees with what I'm about to tell you, and you're welcome to doubt my opinion. However, I am about to make your life easier, so . . .

Ending a Sentence with a Preposition

Winston Churchill is often credited with saying that ending a sentence with a preposition is something "up with which I will not put." Even if he didn't say it, the sarcasm drives home the point that the preposition controversy is, quite simply, silly.

The preposition rule stems from Latin grammar; however, the English language doesn't behave the same way Latin does. Therefore, forcing English to comply with this rule makes no sense. With that in mind, feel free to end sentences with any words you want.

We asked him where he's from.
What is the story about?

Wait, check that. Even though you may feel free to end sentences with prepositions, you should still think about what you're saying and consider whether or not the preposition is the right choice. Sometimes we end on prepositions that are redundant and unnecessary. In these cases, ending with a preposition should be avoided. And sometimes there's simply a better way to say it. Don't end with a preposition just because you can.

Where are you at? **means the same as** Where are you?

Who is the message from?
means the same as
Who sent the message?

Split Infinitives

First you must understand what an infinitive is, then we can discuss why "splitting" one isn't necessarily a horrible thing.

An infinitive verb is the principal, or original, form of a verb: wonder, speak, notice, have. To this verb is added the word *to*: to wonder, to speak, to notice, to have. That's an infinitive.

A split infinitive is one in which an adverb or adverbial phrase is placed between *to* and the infinitive verb: to silently wonder, to bravely speak, to never notice, to always have.

Sometimes splitting an infinitive allows the text to read more smoothly or even to have more impact. Consider this classic line from *Star Trek:* to boldly go where no man has gone before. How much less effective would that line be without the split infinitive? To go boldly where no man has gone before? Or, even worse, *boldly to go?* [shudder] No thanks.

Of course, since you'll be avoiding adverbs from now on, split infinitives shouldn't be too much of a problem. But when it really feels right, split away.

Singular *They* (and *Their* and *Them*)

They is often used as a singular pronoun when the gender of the person being referenced is unknown or when the writer doesn't want to specify.

One of the problems with the English language, unlike many other languages, is that there is no singular gender-nonspecific pronoun *for people.* The masculine pronouns *he, his,* and *him* used to be standard for gender-nonspecific writing, but that usage is largely considered sexist now. The use of *he or she, him/her, his or hers,* and the like has issues as well. When used too much, these constructions can be wordy, distracting, and even confusing. And should you use *he/she* or *she/he*? Depending on your audience, implied sexism (by always putting the masculine pronoun first) can again be a problem. Some authors have tried switching back and forth (masculine pronoun first, then feminine pronoun first, then masculine, then feminine, and so on), and I can tell you from experience that it's awful. Please don't ever write like that. It's a terrible thing to do to readers.

According to *Merriam-Webster*, "*they* has been in consistent use as a singular pronoun since the late 1300s."[1] How or why this usage became demonized is a mystery to me. Regardless, in today's linguistic climate, the singular *they* is acceptable, so don't be afraid to use it.

For example:

Someone knocked at the door, but when I answered, they were gone.
Since the identity of the knocker is unknown, *they* is used as the gender-nonspecific pronoun.

Any true fan would give their eyeteeth to see that band live.
Since the gender could be male or female or nonbinary, *they* is an all-inclusive, nonspecific pronoun.

A Word about Gender Identity

Speaking of all-inclusive, many folks in the world identify as nonbinary (neither male nor female). If you're writing fiction, you probably know how your characters identify. However, if you're writing nonfiction, you may run into questions. Use of the singular *they* not only allows you to be inclusive but also helps you to avoid misidentifying people whose gender identity you simply don't know.

Incomplete Sentences

We all know that a complete sentence includes a subject and a verb and that it expresses a complete thought. Simply using a capital letter at the beginning and appropriate punctuation at the end is not enough to qualify for "complete sentence" status.

Complete Sentence:
When they opened the box, they stared in disbelief at the treasure they had found.

Incomplete Sentences:
When they opened the box. (*not a complete thought*)
The treasure they had found. (*not a complete thought*)

None of this is in dispute.

What may be disputable, however, is whether using an incomplete sentence is actually *wrong*. Particularly in creative writing, a well-placed incomplete sentence can have a lot of impact. Consider the difference between these two examples:

She crept on tiptoes, white-knuckling her grasp on the flashlight until she reached the bottom of the stairs.

She crept on tiptoes, white-knuckling her grasp on the flashlight. Until she reached the bottom of the stairs.

What's the difference between those two examples other than sentence structure? Impact. Suspense. Just separating that clause as its own sentence, albeit an incomplete one, gives that thought so much more oomph.

Starting a Sentence with a Coordinating Conjunction

Coordinating conjunctions live to link things together. That means that these words have to be in the middle somewhere. Put one at the beginning of the sentence, and there is simply no linking going on at all. This is a big, bad no-no.

Or is it? (See what I did there?) When you start with a coordinating conjunction, technically all you're doing is creating an incomplete sentence, which we've already established can be very effective.

> She gave all her effort, and she surpassed expectations.
> She gave all her effort. And she surpassed expectations.

Along with adding impact, as with the example above, coordinating conjunctions can be effective transition words. I use them in this way all the time, and you'll find numerous examples of this usage throughout this book. Just check out the last sentence in this section.

> Most of the neighborhood boys liked to take over the practice field on Saturdays. And then there was Charlie.

Use a coordinating conjunction at the beginning of a sentence only when it adds impact or creates a smooth transition between sentences. Overuse can become tedious, so don't overdo it. But when the time is right, go for it.

Using Comma Splices

The comma splice occurs when two independent clauses are joined by a comma and no coordinating conjunction. In this situation, a semicolon is the grammatically correct solution, but it's been determined by someone somewhere that the comma splice is perfectly OK to use from time to time in narrative writing. I'll try to curb my sarcasm. Here's an example:

The comma splice is wrong, *it's just so wrong!*

The comma splice is wrong **and** it's just so wrong **are** both independent clauses that can stand on their own, but I've shoved them together using a comma instead of a semicolon and with no coordinating conjunction. That's what makes it a comma splice.

The comma splice is acceptable when **all three** of the following conditions apply:

1. The two sentences being combined are *very* closely related to each other. AND

2. Use of a conjunction obstructs the flow of the narrative or just doesn't sound right. AND

3. Using a semicolon is "too formal."

I'll be honest with you here, because we're friends—I don't get it. The "too formal" designation that's been given to the semicolon doesn't make sense to me. It's a punctuation mark, not a prom dress—a punctuation mark with *very few* purposes in the English language, and the biggest one of them is to connect independent clauses that are joined without a coordinating conjunction. So when you use a comma splice, you're effectively slashing over 50 percent of the semicolon's income and leaving the poor thing destitute and unwanted.

Now ask me whether, when I'm copyediting fiction and narrative nonfiction, I let my authors get away with using the occasional comma splice. Go ahead. Ask me. The answer is yes. Yes, I do. And it makes my left eye twitch. But I do it! I do it because, even though I don't see the value in the comma splice, it has become an acceptable "error" in narrative writing.

So if you want to sprinkle your fiction or narrative nonfiction with comma splices—and by sprinkle, I mean *don't use them very often* (on this point, just about everyone agrees)—then you should be fine to do so. You might mention to your copy editor that you prefer using the comma splice now and then so that your editor doesn't try to change them.

Also, use of the comma splice should be *intentional*. Don't use it just because you can. Similar to ending a sentence with a preposition, if you do it, there should be a reason, and it should be the most appropriate option.

Chapter 5

Commonly Misused Words

Many words are easy to confuse or mix up. Keeping straight the difference between *effect* and *affect* or *imply* and *infer* can make your head spin. This chapter will help you navigate many of these difficult-to-remember definitions and usages.

NOTE: Many of these words have multiple definitions. Only the definition that causes confusion is addressed here.

Advice/Advise

Advice is a noun meaning guidance. **Advise** is a verb meaning to give guidance.

> She offered her unsolicited advice.
>
> He advised them against breaking the rules.

All/Both

Use **all** when referring to more than two. Use **both** when referring to only two.

> All three sisters attended NYU.
>
> Both twins moved to Chicago.

Among/Between

In most situations, **among** refers to more than two, while **between** refers to only two. And while *between* can often be used for more than two, never use *among* for fewer than three.

> They dispersed the prize money among the four of them.
>
> The boy sat between his parents.

Amount/Number

Amount refers to volume. **Number** refers to count. *(See chapter 6 for more information.)*

> An amount of water
>
> A number of buckets

Assume

To **assume** means to draw a conclusion based on little to no information, but we often use this word when we actually mean *conclude, reason, understand, ascertain, infer,* or even *gather.* If there is information from which to extrapolate a conclusion, then the person isn't assuming.

Incorrect: I saw the message and the boxes and assumed I was supposed to unpack them.

Correct: I saw the message and the boxes and concluded I was supposed to unpack them.

NOTE: The definition does not imply accuracy or inaccuracy. Assumptions aren't always wrong (and conclusions based on information aren't always right).

Bad/Badly

Bad is an adjective. **Badly** is an adverb.

They felt bad about the joke.
He was badly injured in the accident.

NOTE: If you say you "feel badly," you're actually saying that either you have a faulty sense of touch or you're not good at physically reaching out to touch something. (*Learn more in chapter 8.*)

Cement/Concrete

Cement is one of the ingredients in concrete. **Concrete** is the stuff basement floors and sidewalks are made from.

This concrete doesn't have enough cement in it.
They poured the new concrete patio yesterday.

Compel/Impel

To be **compelled** means to be pushed into something through force or pressure. To be **impelled** means to be persuaded for moral or ethical reasons.

His mother had long since compelled him to avoid using drugs
The veteran's speech impelled her to support the cause.

Complement/Compliment

Complement means to enhance. **Compliment** means to flatter.

> Her necklace complemented her outfit.
>
> The guests complimented her impeccable sense of style.

Could of / Would of / Should of

These phrases are confusing because "could've," "would've," and "should've" *sound* like they use *of* instead of the contraction for *have*. But that's simply not correct. Replace *of* with *have*: *could have / would have / should have.*

Council/Counsel

Council means an assembly of persons for advisory or legislative purposes. **Counsel** means advice (noun) or to give advice (verb).

> The governor consulted his council.
>
> The governor was in need of counsel.
>
> The committee counseled the governor.

Different From Versus Different Than

In American English, the correct phrase is **different from**. However, **differently than** is often acceptable.

> Your coat is different from mine.
>
> That dress hangs on you differently than it does on me.

Emigrate/Immigrate

You **emigrate** from somewhere. You **immigrate** to somewhere.

> He emigrated from Italy.
>
> They immigrated to the US.

Enormity/Magnitude

Enormity and magnitude do not mean the same thing. **Magnitude** means to have great significance. **Enormity** means hugeness or *extreme evil* (that's an interesting range of meanings!).

They were stunned by the enormity of the hole.

They were stunned by the enormity of her crime.

They were silenced by the magnitude of the occasion.

NOTE: In the first edition, I did not include the definition "hugeness" for *enormity*, and I honestly can't say whether I just missed this definition or it didn't exist at that time. But even with this definition, you can see that *enormity* and *magnitude* are quite different.

Ensure/Insure

To **ensure** means to guarantee. To **insure** means to take out insurance on.

He ensured their safety.

He insured their house.

Farther/Further

Farther refers to physical distance. **Further** refers to time or degree or other measures of distance.

They traveled farther than ever before.

She furthered the study of genetics.

Fewer/Less

Fewer is a count comparison. **Less** is a volume comparison. (*See chapter 6 for more information.*)

He had fewer buckets.

He had less water.

Flesh Out / Flush Out

Flesh out means to give substance to. **Flush out** means to cleanse or to expose.

> He fleshed out the main character's past.
> He flushed out the wound with warm water.
> The dogs flushed out the ducks for the hunters.

Former/Latter

In terms of lists, **former** means first, and **latter** means second (of two) or last.

> Between french fries and mashed potatoes, she preferred the former [french fries] over the latter [mashed potatoes].

Good/Well

Good is an adjective. **Well** is usually an adverb but acts as an adjective when referring to health.

> This is good coffee.
> He finished well ahead of the rest. (**adverb**)
> I don't feel well. (**adjective—use only when referring to health**)

NOTE: When someone asks how you are, answering "I'm good" means your life or situation is in good shape, while answering "I'm well" means that you're in good health.

Historic/Historical

Historic refers to something important. **Historical** refers to something from the past.

> She made a historic discovery.
> She wrote a historical fiction novel.

NOTE: Some people use the indefinite article *an* with words like *historic* and *historical* (and many other words beginning with *h*), but that's not technically correct in *American* English. Unless the *h* is not pronounced at all (like with *honor*), you should always use the indefinite article *a*, not *an*.

Imply/Infer

To **imply** means to suggest. To **infer** means to interpret.

She implied her intent to leave.

He inferred she was joking.

HINT: The speaker implies. The listener infers.

Instinct/Instinctive/Instinctual

An **instinct** is something inherent—something you're born with. We often say that someone is thinking, feeling, or acting instinctually; however, humans have few instincts, if any (depends on who you ask). So when you're trying to describe someone acting, thinking, or feeling without a second thought, describe it as *automatic, reflexive, spontaneous, unconscious,* or something similar. But rarely is it correct to describe it as an instinct because almost everything we do, think, or feel is learned (regardless of what the thesaurus says).

She automatically knew what to do to avoid the crash.

Within minutes of being born, the colt instinctively tried to get to its feet.

Lay/Lie

Lay means to set something down. **Lie** means to recline.

Go lay the book on the shelf.

I need to lie down.

And to make it even more confusing, the past tense of *lie* is *lay*: Yesterday, I lay in the grass for hours.

Nauseous/Nauseated

Over time, continued usage has modified how these words are used, and their meanings are basically the same now. The only real difference at this point is that **nauseous** is an adjective and **nauseate** is a verb (the participle forms, *nauseating* and *nauseated*, can also be used as adjectives).

The roller-coaster ride made me feel nauseous.

The roller-coaster ride made me feel nauseated.

Roller-coaster rides nauseate me.

Passed/Past

Passed is the past tense of the verb *pass*. **Past** can be an adjective, adverb, preposition, or noun, but is never a verb.

I passed her on the street. (**verb**)

He believes in past lives. (**adjective**)

I ran past. (**adverb**)

It is past midnight. (**preposition**)

The past is dead. (**noun**)

Peak/Peek/Pique

Peak refers to an apex. **Peek** is a verb meaning to sneak a look. **Pique** is most often used as a verb meaning to stimulate.

They reached the peak of Mount Kilimanjaro.

Peek around the corner and let me know what's going on.

That'll certainly pique their curiosity.

NOTE: For this definition, *pique* is pronounced like *peek*. If you pronounce it "peekay," you're using a completely different definition.

Rack/Wrack

These words are often interchangeable but do have distinct meanings. **Rack** means "to cause to suffer torture, pain, anguish, or ruin."[1] It also means to accumulate. **Wrack** means to wreck or ruin.

She racked (**or wracked**) her brain for the answer.

He was racked (**or wracked**) with pain after the fall.

They had racked up quite a bit of debt.

Lex Luthor wracked Metropolis. (**If you think this one sounds odd, that's because it's not a common usage. But see** *reek/wreak*.)

Reek/Wreak

Reek means to emanate (like an odor). **Wreak** means to cause something.

The house reeks of fish.

Lex Luthor wreaked destruction on Metropolis.

Set/Sit

Set means to lay something down. **Sit** means to be seated.

Set down those papers and come here.

Sit in that chair and wait.

Tortuous/Torturous

Tortuous means winding (like a path) or devious/tricky. **Torturous** means painful or unpleasant (like torture).

His tortuous ways left her with lingering trust issues.

Our trip was plagued by torturous flight delays.

Who/Whom

Who is a pronoun in the nominative case, and **whom** is a pronoun in the objective case. In other words, *who* is a subject, and *whom* is an object.

He wondered who would be there.
(*Who* is the subject of the clause "who would be there.")

For whom the bell tolls
(*Whom* is the object of the preposition *for*.)

He wondered whom he would be seeing.
(*Whom* is the object of the verb "would be seeing.")

HINT: If your clause already has a subject, use *whom* (she knew whom she should ask for help). If your clause has no other subject, use *who* (she knew who could help her).

Or—and this hurts me a little—just use *who* for everything. *Whom* is gradually being phased out and unless you're writing high-minded literary fiction, you can probably get away with not using *whom* at all (and letting your copy editor fix any problematic usages).

Comparative Words

Better/Best
Less/Least
More/Most
Worse/Worst
-Er/-Est

Better, less, more, worse, and adjective forms ending in the suffix **-er** (clearer, larger) are comparative adjectives used when talking about *only two* things. **Best, least, most, worst,** and adjective forms ending in the suffix **-est** (clearest, largest) are superlative adjectives used when talking about *more than two* things and for expressing an extreme in the comparison.

The less/more dominant twin (comparing only two things)

The best/worst conditions for swimming (comparing more than two things)

Commonly Confused Spellings

Beside/Besides

Beside means to be next to something. **Besides** means other than, along with, and furthermore.

They sat beside each other.

I wouldn't do this for anyone besides you.

Besides you, I would also do this for my mom.

Besides, I would do this no matter who it was for.

Foreword/Forward

A **foreword** is an introduction to a book usually written by someone other than the author. **Forward** is an adjective meaning a direction that is straight ahead.

The foreword was written by Stephen King.

Keep moving forward to reach your goals.

Its/It's

Its is a possessive pronoun. **It's** is the contraction for *it is*.

She didn't like its color.

It's cold outside.

Loose/Lose

Loose is an adjective meaning not tight. **Lose** is a verb meaning to not win.

The lid was loose.

I always lose at chess.

Reign/Rein

Reign means to rule over. **Rein** means to control (usually via reins, as a horse).

Her power reigned supreme.

The teacher reined in her out-of-control class.

Than/Then

Than is a conjunction or preposition usually expressing some sort or level of comparison. **Then** is an adverb, noun, or adjective often relating to time, order, or consequence.

She is smarter than I am.

Go to the dentist, then pick up the dry cleaning.

There/They're/Their

There can be used as a pronoun, adverb, adjective, and more. **They're** is the contraction for *they are*. **Their** is a possessive pronoun.

The house is over there.

They're not home.

Their house is beautiful.

Whose/Who's

Whose can be an adjective or a pronoun. **Who's** is the contraction for *who is*.

Whose car is that?

Who's in the car?

Your/You're

Your is a possessive pronoun. **You're** is the contraction for *you are*.

Your car is for sale?

You're making a mistake.

Gender-Specific Spellings

Some languages assign gender to, well, just about everything. It's called grammatical gender, but it has nothing to do with actual gender. It's just a way of categorizing nouns.[2] Two of the languages that do this are Latin and French and, as you may know, they are among the biggest influencers on the formation of the modern English language.

One way that grammatical gender is expressed is through spelling. In French, an *e* is added at the end of feminine forms of words, including names. For example, Michel is masculine while Michele is feminine.

For French words that have been incorporated into the English language, the use of these gender-specific spellings has waned over time, most recently because of gender identity awareness and the goal to be as gender neutral as possible to avoid alienating anyone.

Personally, I'm old school. I like the gender-specific spellings because they're true to the language of origin. And I don't think that it's negative or offensive to use these spellings as long as you use them to indicate the gender that the person identifies as.

The masculine spellings are considered generic or gender-nonspecific, so anyone identifying as male or nonbinary would use the masculine/generic spelling. Anyone identifying as female would use the feminine spelling.

You might not agree with this, and that's totally OK. If you prefer, use masculine/generic spellings across the board when dealing with words like the following.

Blond/Blonde

Protégé/Protégée

Hey, even if you drop the gender spellings, don't forget those accent marks!

Exception: Fiancé/Fiancée

For whatever reason, this term continues to maintain its separate spellings, which does not seem to be problematic from an inclusion or sensitivity standpoint. Here's what The Association of LGBTQ+ Journalists has to say about it in their list of terminology: "Acceptable for engaged individuals before marriage. Gender-neutral options include engaged partner, person, or couple."[3]

Nonexistent Words and Irregular Words to Avoid

Ala Carte/Ala Mode

"Ala" is not a word. These are French phrases and are correctly spelled as three words (with a grave accent [`] over the first *a*):

à la carte
à la mode

Alot

A lot is *always* two words. (The word meaning "to give out a share of something" is spelled *allot*.)

Alright

Alright has a somewhat contentious existence. In most circumstances, it's perfectly acceptable. However, you may run into editors and publishers who insist on the more widely approved original spelling, *all right*.

Anyways

Drop the *s*. Use *anyway*.

Conversate

The correct word is *converse*.

Enroute

Another French phrase, *en route* is two words (*en* meaning *on* and *route* meaning *the way*).

NOTE: The French *en* is not pronounced the way it looks. Pronounce it like its English counterpart, *on* (this isn't precisely accurate, but it's much better than pronouncing it "n").

Imbed

Like *alright*, *imbed* is actually a word; however, it's a variant of *embed*. To avoid possible issues, just use *embed*.

Irregardless

Use *regardless* or *irrespective*.

Nother

Ever use the phrase "a whole nother"? (e.g., "That's a whole nother problem.") It's as if the word *whole* has been planted inside the word *another* (a-whole-nother). But it hasn't. The correct phrase is *a whole other*.

Orientated

Use *oriented* or *orientation*.

Supposably

This is a terrible combination of *supposedly* and *probably*. Use *supposedly*.

American Versus British Spellings

American and British English differ in many ways, including spelling, usage, and meaning. For example, beware using the word *pants* in the UK. The Brits might think you're talking about your underpants! That's a meaning/usage difference though. Spelling differences are generally less embarrassing.

Many British spellings have entered (or, in some cases, reentered) American English. While you're not likely to switch from *curb* to *kerb*, you may prefer *grey* over *gray* or *towards* over *toward*. One spelling is not better than the other, and you can choose for yourself which you prefer. I lean toward American spellings, yet I much prefer *dialogue* to *dialog* and *aesthetic* to *esthetic* (*aesthetic* is so much prettier!). Use whichever spellings suit you, but be aware that your copy editor may change any UK spellings to American spellings, so be sure to make your preferences known up front. And for the love of Pete, please be consistent!

Also know that there are exceptions to every rule. The spelling differences in the following two lists (especially the second list) are merely guidelines.

American	British
afterward	afterwards
backward	backwards
canceled	cancelled
canceling	cancelling
check	cheque
checker	chequer
downward	downwards
draft	draught

esthetic	aesthetic
forward	forwards
gray	grey
inward	inwards
licorice	liquorice
outward	outwards
percent	per cent
plow	plough
theater	theatre
toward	towards
upward	upwards

Did you notice a pattern with those -ward/-wards words?

Common differences between American and British spellings include the following word endings:

American	British	Examples
-or	-our	valor / valour
-ize	-ise	realize / realise
-er	-re	theater / theatre
-og	-ogue	catalog / catalogue
-yze	-yse	analyze / analyse
-ense	-ence	defense / defence
-ed	-t	dreamed / dreamt
-ll	-l	instill / instil

Ever notice that the US's founding documents, like the Declaration of Independence and the Constitution use British spellings ("to provide for a common defence")? Can you tell we were under British rule back then?

Choose the Correct Word

See answers on page 223.

1. "That sweater [complements/compliments] your eyes beautifully."

   Her [complement/compliment] made me smile.
2. I need to [flesh out/flush out] the plot for my new book.

   The police set up a sting in order to [flesh out/flush out] the suspect.
3. The [amount/number] of people at the party was too much for the [amount/number] of space to hold them.
4. After the garage sale, I had [fewer/less] tchotchkes and [fewer/less] debt.
5. Preserving the [historic/historical] site turned out to be a [historic/historical] decision.
6. What you [implied/inferred] from my speech is not at all what I [implied/inferred].
7. Please [ensure/insure] that you fully [ensure/insure] your belongings.
8. We don't have much [farther/further] to go.

   A degree can help you take your career even [farther/further].
9. I felt [nauseous/nauseated] after eating too much ice cream.
10. To do jazz hands, you need to move [all/both] hands and [all/both] ten fingers.
11. There is great camaraderie [among/between] the members of the group.

    I can't decide [among/between] the red and the blue.
12. He struggled to deal with the [enormity/magnitude] of his loss.

13. Although he felt [compelled/impelled] to stay anonymous, his conscience [compelled/impelled] him to report the crime.
14. She saw the Statue of Liberty in 1948 when her family [emigrated/immigrated] to the US.
15. The house [lays/lies] at the end of the street where they're currently [laying/lying] new asphalt.
16. She motioned to me and said, "[Set/Sit] those things down and come [set/sit] with me for a while."
17. She doesn't sit on the [council/counsel] anymore, but she still [councils/counsels] the mayor on a regular basis.
18. The kids ran [passed/past] us, and on their way they [passed/past] the food truck that sits just [passed/past] the library.
19. Their [tortuous/torturous] scheme left us all feeling a [tortuous/torturous] sense of dread.
20. I can't decide between the cheese soup and garden salad. The [former/latter] sounds hearty and delicious, but the [former/latter] is so much healthier.
21. If you'll allow me to [advice/advise] you, I think you'll find my [advice/advise] to be very helpful.
22. Let's [cement/concrete] the plan before we start mixing the [cement/concrete].
23. I don't feel very [good/well] today, so it's a [good/well] thing that I don't have to go to work.
24. The kitchen [reeked/wreaked] of onions and garlic, which [reeked/wreaked] havoc on our dinner party.
25. If your curiosity is [peaked/peeked/piqued], then [peak/peek/pique] through the window and experience the [peak/peek/pique] of bad decorating.
26. She was [racked/wracked] with guilt after she inadvertently [racked/wracked] the celebration with her outburst.

27. It's appropriate for you to feel [bad/badly] over your inappropriate behavior.

28. Ask the manager [who/whom] has the black vest on if he knows [who/whom] we should give our coats to.

29. Of the two candidates, I can't decide which one is [better/best] and which is [worse/worst]. Although, when there were seven candidates, I knew exactly which one I liked [less/least].

30. If the rope comes [loose/lose], you'll [loose/lose] the wagon.

31. [Its/It's] not clear if the dog ran away or if it lost [its/it's] way.

32. Over [their/there/they're] is where the Bakers are putting [their/there/they're] pool, and [their/there/they're] inviting the whole neighborhood once it's ready.

33. I see [your/you're] finally selling [your/you're] old beat-up car.

34. [Who's/Whose] coming with Alan to the surprise party, and [who's/whose] car are they driving?

35. Red is a better color for me [than/then] blue, so I'm going to buy this red shirt, [than/then] return the blue one I bought yesterday.

36. In order to [reign/rein] effectively, a king must learn to [reign/rein] in his ego.

37. [Beside/Besides] not wanting to be at the game, Amber was also annoyed at having to sit [beside/besides] Gary.

38. One she'd received the [forward/foreword], she was ready to push [forward/foreword] and self-publish her first book.

Chapter 6

Volume Versus Count

Both are quantities, right? Does it really matter which words you use to describe them?

You're asking an editor? Of course it does!

What Is the Difference?

When we talk about volume, we're talking about words that cannot be broken down into individual units: water, music, courage.

With count, however, we're talking about words that *are* individual units: teardrop, song, act.

How to Tell the Difference

There are three quick and easy ways to identify volume words versus count words:

1. **Count words can be counted.** You cannot count water, but you can count teardrops (difficult though it may be).
2. **Most volume words do not have a plural form.** *Musics*, no. *Songs*, yes.
3. **Most volume words cannot take an indefinite article (*a, an*).** A courageous act, but not a courage.

Consider the words *greenery* and *leaf*.

Greenery is what's known as a mass noun and refers to an undefined amount of foliage. Greenery cannot be counted and the word has no plural form. *Greenery* is a volume word.

Leaf is a common noun that refers to an individual unit of foliage. Obviously, *leaf* does have a plural form and, while it may be tedious, leaves can be counted. *Leaf* is a count word.

NOTE: Some words can be both volume words and count words, like *joy* or *fear*. The way you use them defines which type of word they are:

I'm full of joy. (**volume**)

My joys are many. (**count**)

Volume and Count Words

To reiterate the explanations from chapter 5 ...

Amount/Number

When referring to volume, use *amount*. When referring to count, use *number*.

> The arbor was flush with a large amount of greenery.
> The arbor was flush with a large number of leaves.

Less/Fewer

Less is a volume comparison. *Fewer* is a count comparison.

> The arbor has less greenery this year.
> The arbor has fewer leaves this year.

Chapter 7

Punctuation Dos and Don'ts

While punctuation is the realm of the copy editor and proofreader, a working knowledge of some common rules can help you with your own editing and can limit how much your editor or proofreader has to do for you (which will save you time in the long run and could even save you some money).

And before you ask, yes, "dos and don'ts" is correct. See the section on apostrophes.

As a writer, you may think that learning proper punctuation is not important. And honestly, I think that's fair, as long as you promise to hire a *fantastic* editor. The fact is, I'm not sharing these rules so that you feel obligated to master them. I'm sharing these rules *in case you want to* master them. Some of the rules might make perfect sense to you, while others might make your eyes cross. So take from this chapter what you will.

Before you do, though, please note that many punctuation rules are strictly a matter of style and can vary from guide to guide; therefore, some editors may follow different rules. There isn't anything wrong with that, as long as you're consistent.

Quotation Marks

Before we get into the next section, a quick overview of double versus single quotation marks:

In *American* English, double quotation marks are used for dialogue, direct quotations, titles that are not italicized, and the like. Single quotation marks are used for quotations and titles within another quotation or within dialogue. (British English is pretty much the exact opposite, with exceptions.)

Double Quotation Marks:

"It's still raining," Grace said as she stared at the swing set in the backyard.
John Lennon plays harmonica on the Beatles' classic "Love Me Do."
Douglas Adams once said, "I love deadlines. I love the whooshing
   noise they make as they go by."

With Single Quotation Marks:

Margaret said, "We need a sign over the register that says, 'Pay Here.'"
Carlos held up the magazine. "Did you read 'How to Afford Practically
Anything'? Maybe we *can* take that vacation."

Punctuation with Quotation Marks

Do those pesky punctuation marks go inside or outside the quotation marks? Here's the answer.

NOTE: The rules are the same for both single and double quotation marks.

Periods and Commas: Inside

"I'm so bored," Pamela said.
It turns out Hemingway never said, "Write drunk. Edit sober," but it still
seems like good advice.
"I read a great article called 'How to Beat the Wintertime Blues.'"

The exceptions are so few and so specific that it is unlikely you will ever run into one. Therefore, go ahead and think of this as a hard-and-fast rule.

Colons and Semicolons: Outside

It's not that I don't like "Eight Days a Week"; I just like "I Wanna Hold
Your Hand" better.

Question Marks, Exclamation Points, Dashes, Ellipses: Depends

They go *inside* if they are directly connected to the text being quoted.
They go *outside* the quotation marks if they are connected to the sentence as a whole.

Terry asked without much interest, "When will Dad be home?"
The question mark goes with the quoted text, so it is inside the quotation marks.

Do you know the words to "Let It Be"?
The question mark goes with the sentence, not the quoted text, so it is outside the quotation marks.

No, but I know all the words to "Help!"
The exclamation point is part of the song title, so it goes inside the quotation marks.

NOTE: As in the first and last examples, even when the final punctuation mark is inside the quotation mark (meaning it goes with the quoted material, not the sentence as a whole), no other ending punctuation is required.

Space After Punctuation

All punctuation marks require *only one space* after them. If you were trained in a high school typing class to use two spaces between sentences or after colons, stop it! Retrain yourself right now and never, ever hit that space bar twice in a row again.

OK, not everyone agrees with this rule. Some people are pretty passionately against it, and you may well feel the same way. So feel free, in your everyday life, to go nuts with the double spaces. Emails? Product reviews? Chain letters? Live it up. But if you're typing something to be published, industry standard is what it is. If you want your self-published book to look professional (and I know you do or you wouldn't be reading this chapter), follow the one-space rule. (If you don't, your editor—if they know what they're doing—will change it anyway.)

Commas

Before we talk about commas, there are two concepts that will help you: *restrictive* and *nonrestrictive* words, phrases, and clauses.

Restrictive: The word, phrase, or clause furthers the meaning of whatever it modifies and is therefore essential to understanding the sentence.[1]

Nonrestrictive: The word, phrase, or clause is extra information and can be removed from the sentence without changing or obscuring the meaning of the sentence.[2]

Keep in mind that when I'm talking about the importance of the information, I mean in a grammatical sense, not in terms of the story itself. In other words, just because the information isn't essential *to the sentence* doesn't mean it isn't important to the story.

To illustrate restrictive versus nonrestrictive, let's say I have four brothers, and one of them is named Bill. He just had a birthday and I gave him a pretty darn great gift. I might say this:

I gave my brother Bill an amazing birthday present.

Now let's say I have only one brother, still named Bill, with recent birthday and a darn great gift from me. I could say this:

I gave my brother, Bill, an amazing birthday present.

The only difference between these sentences is the commas. Why is that?

In the first example, I have multiple brothers, and if I don't tell you which one I'm talking about, you'll be confused. Therefore, my brother's name is restrictive information. You need to have it in order for the sentence to make sense. It's essential.

In the second example, I have only one brother, so mentioning his name is unnecessary to the meaning of the sentence. Obviously it's Bill. He's the only brother I have. In this case, the information is nonrestrictive. It's nonessential. It's extra.[3]

A restrictive word, phrase, or clause is generally *not* set off by commas. Nonrestrictive words, phrases, and clauses generally *are* set off by commas.

OK, let's talk comma usage.

In a Series . . .

This is perhaps the most contentious punctuation rule, oh, ever. It's known in the editing biz as the serial comma or Oxford comma (referencing a usage rule set forth by Oxford University a really, really, *really* long time ago). If you follow *Chicago* style, you will use the Oxford comma. If you follow AP style, you won't. If you don't have a preference, you can let your editor decide. If you do have a preference, make sure you let your editor know. (Keep in mind that most publishers have a non-negotiable house style, so unless you self-publish, you likely won't have a choice where this rule is concerned.)

Since we're following *Chicago* style: In a series of three or more items that are combined at the end by a conjunction, use a comma before the conjunction.[4]

> She packed her shampoo, conditioner, and mousse but forgot her hair spray.
> Nathan likes to spend time hiking, whitewater rafting, and swimming.

If a conjunction is used between each item in the series, commas are not required.

> Mary decorated the yard in a ghoulish mix of ghosts and spiders and witches.

In Compound Sentences . . .

As we discussed previously, an independent clause is a sentence that can stand on its own (it contains a complete thought). When two independent clauses are connected by a coordinating conjunction (*and, but,* etc.), you have a compound sentence, and a comma should be used before the conjunction.

April bought plenty of snacks, but she forgot to stock up on soda.
The clouds dissipated around midnight, and stars blanketed the sky.

There are variations on this rule, but this basic tenet will get you by in most cases.

In Complex Sentences . . .

A complex sentence has one independent clause and at least one dependent clause. As you surely remember, a dependent (or "subordinate") clause contains a subordinating conjunction and cannot stand on its own (it's not a complete thought). For example, "if you bring me dinner" is a dependent clause.

(For a list of conjunctions, see appendix B.)

If the dependent clause comes first (i.e., it's the "introductory" clause), use a comma after it.

Although I knew the answer, I kept my mouth shut.
Because she never learned to swim, Karen stayed back from the shore.

However, if the *independent* clause comes first, comma usage varies (and if you aren't already confused, brace yourself):

If the dependent clause furthers the meaning of the independent clause, then no comma is needed.

Barry rarely went to church because his parents had never taken him as a child.

The dependent clause "because his parents had never taken him as a child" further explains the independent clause; therefore, no comma is needed.

If the dependent clause has no real bearing on the independent clause, then a comma should be used.

Barry rarely went to church, although he rather enjoyed himself whenever he did.

The dependent clause "although he rather enjoyed himself whenever he did" is a separate thought and does not further explain the independent clause, so a comma is necessary.

If confusion has thoroughly set in, think about it this way: If the sentence starts with a subordinating conjunction, then you know the dependent clause is first and you should always follow it with a comma. In all other situations, do whatever sounds right to you and let your copy editor sort out the details.

With Relative Clauses (*That* Versus *Which*) . . .

See the glossary for a definition of relative clauses. For now, just know that *that* and *which* are both relative pronouns that introduce relative clauses. How you know which pronoun to use is a bit head-spinning, so let me bottom-line this section first and then you can absorb what you want from the rest of the information.

The bottom line is this: Relative clauses introduced by *which* should be set off by commas. Relative clauses introduced by *that* should not be set off by commas. Here's why:

That typically introduces restrictive clauses, and, as I'm sure you remember, restrictive clauses do not require commas.

Which introduces nonrestrictive clauses. Again, nonrestrictive clauses should be set off by commas.

Now, the first thing you need to determine is whether or not your clause is essential or nonessential to the meaning of the sentence. This will determine which relative pronoun you use: *that* for essential information and *which* for nonessential information. This decision will tell you whether or not to use commas.

Consider these two sentences:

The sliding glass door that Logan installed keeps sticking.
The sliding glass door, which Logan installed, keeps sticking.

Let's say there are multiple sliding glass doors and Logan installed only one of them. We might reference that particular door as "the one Logan installed." This makes the information restrictive. We need it in order to know what door is being referenced. Therefore, we use *that* with no commas (the first example).

However, maybe there's only one sliding glass door and it just so happens to have been installed by Logan. In this case, Logan's involvement is unnecessary information—it's nonrestrictive. Now we have the second example—using *which* and setting it off with commas.

NOTE: In most situations, *that* and *which* are not interchangeable as relative pronouns. *Which* automatically indicates nonessential information is coming. If the information is essential to the meaning of the sentence, use *that*.

With Dates and Addresses . . .

When a full date is given in month-day-year format, the year should be set off by commas:

The Declaration of Independence was ratified on July 4, 1776, and signed by fifty-six delegates.

However, the year is not set off by commas if the day is left out or if the year is combined with a holiday name:

> The Declaration of Independence was ratified in July 1776 and signed by fifty-six delegates.
>
> I remember celebrating the bicentennial on Independence Day 1976.

Similarly, the names of states and countries are set off by commas in an address:

> She lives in Hartford, Connecticut, in a beautifully restored brownstone.
>
> We visited Lyon, France, on our European tour.

Note, though, that in a full address including zip code, the comma that would normally follow the state name is moved to after the zip code.

> The post office is located at 123 North Fielding Street, Bancroft, MN 82749, next to the hardware store.

When Addressing Someone Directly (Like in Dialogue) . . .

A comma should come before and after the name of someone being directly addressed.

> "Lynn, please bring me my phone."
>
> "Hey, Lynn, will you please bring me my phone?"
>
> "Hi, honey, I'll be home in about an hour."

Before Quoted Text . . .

In most cases, you should use a comma before quoted text.

Elaine paced a few times, then said, "I can't believe this happened."

However, if the quoted material is introduced by a conjunction (like *if* or *that*) and thus weaved seamlessly into the text, no comma is needed.

Mom clearly stated that "you better be home by eleven."

Ellipses

Ah, those three little dots that we love to use so much and *so incorrectly*. There are really only two reasons most of us need to use ellipses. I doubt you'll stop there, though, and neither do I (note my subheadings), but *choosing* to break the rules is much better than unknowingly breaking them and I wouldn't try to stop you from making stylistic choices that better serve your art. Still, following are the correct reasons to use ellipses, just so you know.

In quoted text . . .

When there is an omission in quoted text, the ellipsis is used to fill the gap and indicate that copy is missing.

"When there is an omission . . . the ellipsis is used to . . . indicate that copy is missing."

Note that when an ellipsis is used in this way, the resulting text must read as a complete sentence.

In dialogue . . .

When a speaker is faltering (e.g., struggling to put words together or to complete a thought), the breaks in their speaking pattern should be shown through ellipses.

> "I can't quite . . . I mean . . . how do I say this?"
> "I can't quite . . . I mean . . ." *How do I say this?*

When Not to Use Ellipses

Don't use ellipses to trail off a complete thought (see the first and third examples below) or to cut off someone's speech (second example). These are common misuses. When you have a complete thought, just use normal punctuation at the end, and to cut someone off mid-sentence, use an em dash.

These are all incorrect:

> "Please follow me . . ." she instructed.
> "What's wrong with . . . ?" She stopped when he smiled.
> Let's explore some of these options . . .

Use instead:

> "Please follow me," she instructed.
> "What's wrong with—" She stopped when he smiled.
> Let's explore some of these options.

Ellipses with Other Punctuation

With most other punctuation, there should be a space between the punctuation mark and the nearest ellipsis dot. This includes periods at the end of sentences, which should not be omitted. Yes, that means that you could have four periods in a row.

"Is that what I think . . . ?" *(space between ellipsis dot and question mark)*
According to the text, "Always back up files. . . . This will save you a lot of heartbreak." *(space between period and ellipsis dot)*

The exception is with quotation marks. If you have an incomplete thought that does not have its own ending punctuation, the ending quotation mark should immediately follow the last ellipsis dot.

"I can't quite . . . I mean . . ."

How to Create an Ellipsis

You probably do what most people do. You just plop three periods down next to each other, and your word processing program converts them into an ellipsis character. Guess what? That's wrong!*

A proper ellipsis has a space before and after each dot.

This: text . . . text
Not This: text...text
Or This: text... text
Or This: text ... text

The problem with these spaces is what happens when your ellipsis falls at the end of the line and gets split in two—half at the end of one line and the rest at the beginning of the next line. Well, this is tricky. It involves something called a "nonbreaking space," which I don't want to confuse you with here. If you ever run into this problem, you can learn all about nonbreaking spaces online—how they work and how to use them.

*OK, *wrong* is a strong word. Using the ellipsis character is perfectly acceptable if that's what you want to do. Just be aware that it is not in line with *The Chicago Manual of Style*. Also note that,

if you do use the ellipsis character, you need to have a space before and after it (text … text), unless it is immediately followed by a
punctuation mark, in which case there should be no space after the
ellipsis character (text …,).

Hyphens and Dashes

The proper use of hyphens (-), en dashes (–), and em dashes (—)
is complicated, to put it mildly. Overcomplicated, in my opinion. I
could delve into all the ways we misuse hyphens when we should
use an en dash (and there are many) or the myriad uses of the em
dash. But I won't. Just keep doing what you've always done, except
for the following.

Hyphens

One of the biggest misuses of the hyphen is in the making of compound words—or, rather, in *not* making compound words. When
two or more words work together to create a single noun, adjective,
verb, and so on, those words are usually linked by hyphens. We do
pretty well with nouns, but other parts of speech tend to get left
hyphenless.

For example, would you say her all too familiar advice **or** her
all-too-familiar advice? **How about** the rabbit hippity hopped for the
fence **or** the rabbit hippity-hopped for the fence?

In the first example, "all-too-familiar" is a compound adjective.
All three words work together to create a single description; therefore, the words should be hyphenated. Similarly, in the second example, "hippity-hopped" is a compound verb and should also be
hyphenated. (Full disclosure: "Hippity" is not a real word outside
of children's picture books. But you get my point.)

Adding these hyphens can make the copy easier to read and understand, so please don't leave them out. They matter.

NOTE: Compound adjectives are often left open (no hyphens) when they appear *after* the noun they modify. Consider the difference between her all-too-familiar advice **and** her advice is all too familiar to me. If you're unsure, consult the dictionary. If it's hyphenated in the dictionary, hyphenate it both before and after the noun. If it's not hyphenated in the dictionary (or it isn't in the dictionary at all), then hyphenate it before the noun but not after.

ANOTHER NOTE: Adverbs that end in -ly are *never* hyphenated when combined with an adjective, either before or after the noun. For example, his deeply rooted fears, *not* his deeply-rooted fears.

Some words are spelled differently depending on how they function. Consider the word *setup*, which is one word as a noun, two words as a verb, and one hyphenated word as an adjective.

He *set up* his desk just the way he likes it. (**verb**)
The whole evening was nothing but a *setup*. (**noun**)
The design firm's *set-up* fee was outrageous. (**adjective**)

So don't assume that a word is always hyphenated just because it's hyphenated some of the time. Hyphenation can vary depending on how the words function within the sentence and how they relate to one another. Again, consulting the dictionary can help with this issue.

En Dashes

En dashes are generally used in several ways, but the one you're most likely to encounter is the use of the en dash as a stand-in for the word *to* or *through*.

100–150
9 a.m.–5 p.m.
Monday–Friday

While we're used to using hyphens in these constructions, en dashes are easier to read, due to their longer length. Also, if you think of hyphens as connectors for combining two or more words into one, then think of en dashes as connectors that take the place of words (in this case, the words *to* and *through*). This won't explain every prescribed usage of the en dash, but it helps to understand this one.

How to Type an En Dash

If you're working on a Mac, simply type Opt–Hyphen, and you're done. It doesn't matter what software you're using.

If you're working on a PC, I'm very sorry . . .

In Word, you can type Ctrl–Num-Hyphen ("Num-Hyphen" refers to the hyphen on the numeric keypad of a full-size keyboard). Or you can go to Insert>Symbols, choose the Special Characters tab, and insert an en dash.

In Google Docs, go to Insert>Symbols>Special Characters, switch the left-hand dropdown to Punctuation and the right-hand dropdown to Dashes/Connectors, then find the en dash.

In other software, find the Special Characters or Glyphs palette, possibly under the Insert menu, and you should be able to find an en dash.

Em Dashes

There are only two things that you might want, or could possibly need, to know about the em dash.

First, as I showed in the ellipses section, the em dash (not an ellipsis) is used to indicate cutoff speech.

"I can't be—"

The second is the use of the em dash in place of commas, parentheses, and colons. The correct format is to insert the em dash between words with no spaces.

Their preferred colors—blue, orange, and black—are used effectively on their website.

Given his love of suspense thrillers—his favorite topic of conversation—he sat through all twelve hours of the Hitchcock marathon.

Em dashes cause a more abrupt interruption of the text (which explains why they are used to interrupt a speaker). Use the em dash in this way when you want the interruption to have more impact than you get from commas or parentheses.

Here's a fun way to think about the difference between commas, parentheses, and em dashes within sentences.

Commas equal an afterthought = He avoids sugar, which he's totally addicted to, in his cooking.

Parentheses equal a side comment = He avoids sugar (he's totally addicted to it) in his cooking.

Em dashes equal an intrusion = He avoids sugar—because he's totally addicted to it—in his cooking.

The harshness of the interruption increases from commas (the least harsh), to parentheses (second harshest), to em dashes (the harshest).

As a side note, here's something annoying: I'm told by people who use AI a lot (I currently don't use it much at all, so I'm taking their word for it) that AI uses a lot of em dashes, which could have the effect of making people think that if your text uses em dashes, it must have been written by AI. Quite frankly, that's a dumb conclusion, and you should feel free to continue to use em dashes. However, overuse of em dashes could get your writing flagged as being AI generated, whether or not that's true. So at the very least, be sure you're using em dashes only when they are called for and not as a general replacement for other more appropriate punctuation.

How to Type an Em Dash

In most cases, you can just use two hyphens together, and your word processing program should convert them into an em dash for you (although note that Google Docs returns an en dash for some reason).

Otherwise . . .

On a Mac, simply type Opt–Shift–Hyphen. Job done.

On a PC, the process is pretty much the same as for making en dashes, except in Word, type Alt–Ctrl–Num-Hyphen (the hyphen on the numeric keypad).

Colons

A colon is most often used to introduce an idea or a list that further explains or illustrates what is being said.

> She gathered the necessary ingredients: flour, sugar, cocoa, eggs, vanilla, baking soda.
> He decided right then what he must do: testify against the cartel.

A colon can also be used to introduce another sentence that furthers the point in the first sentence, but don't get colons confused with semicolons (see next page).

Also note that the structure to the left of the colon should form a complete sentence.

Correct: Remember to bring these supplies: a pencil, an eraser, and a sketch pad.

Incorrect: Remember to bring: a pencil, an eraser, and a sketch pad.

"Remember to bring" is not a complete sentence. *Bring* is a transitive verb that requires an object, which is missing from the second example. Simply remove the colon to fix the problem.

Furthermore, when two *complete* sentences are connected by a colon, the second sentence should be capitalized.

He decided right then what he must do: He had to testify against the cartel.

Semicolons

You are most likely to use a semicolon in one of two ways:

+ To separate two independent clauses when no conjunction is used
She couldn't take it anymore; she had to move out of her parents' house.

+ In place of commas to separate items in a complex series
Washington, DC, is home to monuments like the Lincoln Memorial, an homage to President Abraham Lincoln; the Vietnam Memorial, which pays tribute to those missing or killed in the Vietnam War; the Washington Monument, which honors Founding Father and first president George Washington; and many others.

As I mentioned previously, there are those who think that semicolons are too formal and who prefer the overly informal (grumble, grumble) comma splice. However, there's nothing wrong with using the semicolon to connect two independent clauses. As I've said, that is the semicolon's job, after all. So there's no need to listen to haters. (But don't overdo it. Use the semicolon between sentences only when you really want the sentences linked—the sentences should be very close in meaning—but don't want to use a conjunction.)

Conjunctive Adverbs and Phrases

Adverbs like *however, therefore,* and *accordingly,* as well as phrases like *that is* and *for example,* are often used like conjunctions, but they require special punctuation. Instead of just a comma before, like with actual conjunctions, precede the adverb/phrase with a semicolon and follow it with a comma.

> The lake was frozen; however, the ice was too thin for skating.
> I never make my bed; therefore, I keep my bedroom door closed when my mom comes over.
> Henry caved pretty easily; that is, his daughter didn't have to work very hard for that new doll.

Apostrophes

Apostrophes are probably the most abused punctuation marks of all time.[5] At some point, a large portion of the population became convinced that the apostrophe should be used to make a word plural. This is *never* the case—not even in a phrase like "dos and don'ts." (Why would you spell it "do's" and then not spell the other word "don'ts"? It makes no sense to use apostrophe *s* on one word but not the other. This is a pretty big clue that the apostrophe is wrong.)

According to *Chicago*, 18th edition rules, the few situations in which an apostrophe is used to make something plural include single lowercase letters, some lowercase abbreviations, and single uppercase letters.[6]

He needs to mind his p's and q's.
Mindy loves her new pj's.
She signed the note with X's and O's.

Uppercase abbreviations, acronyms, and numbers do not require an apostrophe to be made plural. And neither do any words. Ever. I cannot stress this enough. *Never use an apostrophe to make a word plural.*

Correct Usage

The most common and proper uses of the apostrophe are to make nouns possessive and to create contractions. Apostrophes also take the place of missing letters or numbers (like in *the '80s*). Words are made possessive by adding apostrophe *s* or just an apostrophe at the end. Contractions, of course, are the combining of two words into one with an apostrophe filling in for the missing letters from the second word: *it's, you're, he'll.*

That's Sheila's car. (contraction: *that's*; possessive: *Sheila's*)
Ron's dad is a police detective. (possessive: *Ron's*)
He writes children's books for a living. (possessive: *children's*)

Possessive Words Ending in S

When I was growing up, the rule was simple. If a word ended in *s*, the apostrophe followed the *s*. There were no exceptions.

Russ' opinion
The birds' nests

These days, *Chicago* recommends adding apostrophe *s* to singular nouns and an apostrophe only to plural nouns, with some exceptions.

Russ's opinion
The birds' nests

So basically, even if a word ends in an *s*, the possessive is formed by adding an apostrophe *s*—if the word is singular.

Can you believe they towed Gary Banks's car? *(singular—add apostrophe s)*
The Bankses' house is being fumigated this week. *(plural—add apostrophe only)*

This might seem odd to you. I mean, if a word already ends in *s*, why add another one? *Chicago* doesn't really explain it, and the best explanation I can come up with is consistency.

Singular = apostrophe *s*
Plural = apostrophe only
Done.

And then there are the exceptions, which are surprisingly few:
- Words and names that end in an *s* that is not pronounced (like Des Moines) or that is pronounced like a *z* (like Euripides) are made possessive with an apostrophe *s*, even when they're plural (it's a pronunciation thing).
- Nouns that are plural in form but singular in meaning (like *politics*) are treated like plurals and use an apostrophe only.

* Words like *goodness* take an apostrophe only in the phrase *for . . . sake*, which is again a pronunciation thing: Adding an apostrophe *s* also adds an "es" sound to the end of the word, which is a mouthful in a phrase like *for goodness' sake*. Leaving off the extra *s* allows for less complicated pronunciation.[7]

Apostrophes at the Beginning of a Word or Number

When an apostrophe is used at the beginning of a word or number to denote that part of the word or number is missing, the apostrophe should curve *to the left* (like a closing single quotation mark or, you know, *an apostrophe*). Unfortunately, your app is probably going to make it curve to the right (like an *opening* single quotation mark).

Correct: '80s, rock 'n' roll
Incorrect: '80s, rock 'n' roll

Hey, notice those two apostrophes in *rock 'n' roll*? That's right. Apostrophes take the place of missing letters, and *'n'* is missing two: the *a* before the *n* and the *d* after the *n*, hence two apostrophes.

To force a left-curving apostrophe:

On a Mac, use keyboard shortcut Opt Shift–closing bracket (]).

On a PC, find the Special Characters, Glyphs, or Symbols panel and insert the correct character that way. Or type Alt–0146 if you have a numeric keypad on your keyboard.

Or, here's a neat trick. Type any letter plus an apostrophe (a'), then delete the letter. Voilà!

Apostrophes and Quotation Marks Versus Inch and Foot Marks

Wait, there's a difference? Yes, there is!

Apostrophes and quotation marks are curved or slanted (depending on the font). Inch and foot marks are straight up and down or slightly slanted (depending on your font and app). They are *not* interchangeable!

The correct foot mark is called the prime symbol (′), and the correct inch mark is called the double prime symbol (″). It may seem like a silly thing. Everyone's going to understand what you mean, right? But that's like saying that it doesn't matter if you use single or double quotation marks just because they're similar. We're talking about two different sets of marks that are used in very different ways.

Smart Apostrophes and Quotation Marks

Most word processing and other writing programs have a setting called "smart quotes" (or a similar name). This setting tells the program to use curved or slanted marks for apostrophes and quotation marks (again, whether they are curved or slanted depends on the font you're using).

Since we use apostrophes and quotation marks in writing *way* more than we use inch and foot marks, you definitely want to have smart quotes turned on. In fact, it's probably already turned on by default. If it isn't, find it in your Preferences or Settings panel and turn it on.

Making Inch and Foot Marks

For straight up-and-down marks, type the corresponding apostrophe or quotation mark, then use the Undo feature (Cmd–z on a Mac; Ctrl–z on a PC). This should "undo" the smart quote feature and leave you with a straight mark.

" followed by Undo = "

If your program overrides your straight marks and insists on making them into smart quotes (as I've discovered is the case in Apple's Pages program), you may have to turn off smart quotes in Preferences/Settings, make your straight marks, then turn smart quotes back on. Oy! A better option is to use prime symbols instead, as described next.

For the prime symbols, once again it matters if you're on a Mac or a PC. On a Mac, go to the Edit menu and select Emoji & Symbols from the list (available in most apps). Do a search for "prime" and double-click on the symbol to insert it (actually, this method works for all the punctuation marks we've been talking about). On a PC, it matters what software you're in. In Word, go to Insert> Symbol and go to the "General Punctuation" subset to find the prime and double prime characters. If you're in Google Docs, go to Insert>Symbols>Special Characters and do a search for "prime." In other software, look for a "symbols" or "special characters" dialogue box, and you should be able to find the prime characters. (Note that not all fonts include prime characters in their list of special characters.)

The Alternative

I would be remiss if I didn't point out that you can avoid this whole issue with one easy step. Simply spell out "inch/inches" and "foot/feet" instead of using the symbols, which is standard in narrative writing anyway. Problem solved.

What If I'm Typing on My Phone?

It's beyond my understanding why anyone would write on their phone (my snarky side desperately wants to call you crazy). My advice is to stop doing that and work on a device that has an actual keyboard. The problem is that all the same rules apply, but your ability to create any of the special characters I've discussed is seriously stunted. If you insist on using your phone in this way (the joints in your thumbs are very upset with you, by the way), then you'll have to deal with punctuation issues later when editing on a different device.

Part Two

I'm Supposed to Do What Now?

Chapter 8

Odds and Ends

This chapter is filled with issues that aren't big enough or don't take enough time to discuss to warrant their own chapters. They're common peccadillos that many authors, and people in general, struggle with.

Misuse of *Where*

This is one of those times where we can easily get lost.

Have you ever given this type of construction any thought? Why we use *where* in sentences that have nothing to do with location? "One of those times where"—does that make any sense? Consider—

This is one of those *times when* we can easily get lost.
This is one of those *situations in which* we can easily get lost.
This is one of those *places where* we can easily get lost.

The use of *where* in these constructions is often simply habit on the part of a writer who probably learned this usage in childhood and then never gave it a second thought. It seems to make sense on the surface, but in many cases it doesn't fit the meaning of the sentence.

Look at the example sentences above. Note how the conjunctions match in meaning to the words they follow (times *when*, situations [in] *which*, places *where*). This is the key to knowing when it's OK to use *where* and when it isn't.

Unnecessary Quotation Marks

I asked her to marry me, and she said "Yes."

Some authors think that any time they use *say, said,* or a similar word, whatever follows it must be in quotation marks. This is not true. Quotation marks are needed only when you're quoting the character's exact words *as dialogue* or *as an exact quotation,* not when you're just casually reiterating a statement or response. Consider the differences in the two examples that follow.

I asked her to marry me, and she said yes.
I asked her to marry me, and she said, "Why, Charlie Jo Parker, I
would love to marry you!"

In the second example, we're recounting the exact words used in the reply, whereas in the first example, we're simply stating a fact. For this reason, the first example does not require quotation marks.

Here are a few other examples that do not require quotation marks:

He walked in and said hello to everyone.
I know my mom would say no.
Tate said goodbye, then didn't leave for over an hour.

What do these examples have in common? *Yes, no, hello, goodbye,* and a few other similar words can be used as a response or as a *description* of a response. For example, *hello* is something we actually say, but it can also indicate a type of greeting. *Yes* is an actual response, but it can also be a description of a general affirmative response.

Let's look at those same examples but insert different words:

He walked in and said wow to everyone.
I know my mom would say absolutely.
Tate said jeepers, then didn't leave for over an hour.

Wow, absolutely, and *jeepers* are words that don't pull double duty—they can't be used to *describe* a response as well as *being* a response, like *yes* and *hello* can. In these situations, quotation marks are definitely needed. But if you're describing what the person said versus literally quoting them, then quotation marks should be left off.

I knew my mom would say no.
I knew my mom would say "Absolutely!"

(I don't know about you, but I like Mom #2 better!)

Improper Placement of *Only*

Oh boy, do we put this word in the wrong place in sentences, along with its counterpart *just*. I never noticed this until I took a class that pointed out the problem, and now I can't *not* see it! And I'm happy to pass my torment on to you.

Consider this example:

He only wanted to make a difference.

He only *wanted?* As in, he had no other emotions except want? Or perhaps the following would be better?

He wanted only to make a difference.

We tend to put words like *only* in front of verbs instead of where they actually belong in the sentence. Maybe that's because we assume that *only* is an adverb because of its -ly ending. You may recall, however, that way back in chapter 2, I pointed out that *only* can be an adverb *or* an adjective. And that makes the placement of the word all the more difficult, unless you really pay attention to the meaning of the sentence.

She *only* walked to the corner to buy gum.
She walked *only* to the corner to buy gum.
She walked to the corner *only* to buy gum.
She walked to the corner to buy *only* gum.
She walked to the corner to buy gum *only*.

See the differences? With words like *only* and *just,* place them in the sentence next to the precise thing or action that they describe.

You and I Versus You and Me

When I was growing up, people became kind of obsessed with the difference between *me* and *I,* and as people often do, folks went overboard and lost sight of the difference. A lot of people think that "you and me" is always wrong.

Here's an example that, sadly, I don't think I'll ever be able to forget. Back in the '80s, there was a family drama called *Eight Is Enough* that featured Dick Van Patten as the patriarch of a large family (any guesses how large?!) and Willie Aames as his teenage son. Father and son were often at odds, and in one episode in particular, Dad was giving his son trouble about his grades and probably some other stuff that I don't remember. Of course, they patched things up in the neat tied-with-a-bow ending (it was the '80s, after all). Father and son were making plans to do something together that weekend. "Just you and me?" the son asked. With a loving smile, Dad "corrected" him with, "Just you and *I.*"

Wrong! Even as a teenager, I knew the writers got it wrong. [Insert head-slap emoji here.]

To be fair, use of *just* does not determine the pronouns that follow it. Consider the difference between "Just you and I are going to the movie" and "He requested just you and me." *Just* is simply an adjective modifying these pronouns, and it doesn't really care which pronouns you use. But if Willie had used a complete sentence, it would have been something like "You mean it'll be just you and me?"—not "You mean just you and I will go?" (I mean, come on, which one of those sounds like a teenager would say it?)

Besides that, the phrase on its own would never be correct as "just you and I." If you don't believe me, swap the pronouns: "just me and you" or "just I and you"? Yes, indeed, my teenage self got it right. [Insert heel-clicking emoji here.]

With *Between*

Between is a preposition that requires an object. *I* is a subject. *Me* is an object. Bottom line? Never ever use *I* directly after the word *between* (or any other preposition)—always use *me*. (That is *not* just between you and me—spread the word!)

Tricks to Help You Decide

Here are a few tricks to help you figure out which pronoun is correct.

1. **Swap the pronouns.** As I demonstrated, instead of saying "you and me" or "you and I," swap the pronouns. Would you say "between I and you" or "between me and you"? Often, how words *sound* isn't a good indication of what's correct. This is not one of those times. If "between I and you" makes you cringe (and it should), then you know that "between you and I" is also wrong.

2. **Replace with *we* and *us*.** Try the phrase using *we* instead of *you and I* and *us* instead of *you and me*. Would you say "just we" or "just us"? "Between we" or "between us"? You can use this trick to help figure out the correct subject as well ("We went to the store" or "Us went to the store"?). Just remember that *we* is the same as *you and I* and *us* is the same as *you and me*.

3. **Check the function in the sentence.** Are you dealing with the subject of the clause? No? Then you probably shouldn't use *I* since it's a subject, not an object. This trick isn't fool-

proof because sometimes it can be difficult to discern if you need nominative (subject) or objective (object) case. But this is often a reliable test. Hopefully you would never say "You and me are going on a trip" (because you shouldn't!). Just as you shouldn't say "He's taking you and I to the store."

Adjective and Adverb Swapping

All [insert noun here] are created equal.
Don't take it personal.
[Do something] as close as possible.
I feel badly.

All of these are wrong, but a lot of people don't realize it because these faulty constructions are used incorrectly so often that they start to sound correct. And quite frankly, sometimes it's difficult to decide when to use an adjective and when to use an adverb. If you struggle with this, here are some tips:

1. First and foremost, you have to decide what your modifier is modifying. This isn't always easy. In "don't take it personally," which is the correct wording, does the modifier refer to "don't take" (the verb) or to "it"? Well, ask what the modifier is doing. In this case, it's describing one's emotional reaction, not the thing being reacted to (the "it"). Therefore, it modifies the verb and requires an adverb. In cases in which logic doesn't clear it up, you might try a couple of things. First, try rearranging the sentence—"don't personally take it"—and see if it still makes some sense. You might also try removing words—"don't take personally"—and again see if the sentence still works, albeit awkwardly.

2. If you decide that the word being modified is a noun or pro-
    noun, then you know automatically that the modifier has to
    be an adjective. If you decide that the word being modified is
    an adjective or adverb, then the modifier has to be an adverb.

3. If you decide that the word being modified is a verb, you
    have to make another decision: Is it an action verb or a state-
    of-being verb? Action verbs are modified by adverbs. State-
    of-being verbs aren't usually modified at all. Instead they
    link the subject with a word that modifies it, and since sub-
    jects are nouns, that modifier has to be an adjective ("I am
    sorry"—*sorry* modifies *I*, not *am*).

Let's explore the differences between action verbs and their modifiers and state-of-being verbs and their, um, non-modifiers. Let's
start with a classic, as already discussed in chapter 5, "Commonly
Misused Words."

I feel bad. Why, you may still be wondering, is it *bad* instead of
badly? Badly is an adverb, and adverbs modify *action* verbs. But this
sentence indicates an emotion, not an action. That makes *feel* a
state-of-being verb, and that means that our modifier is not modifying the verb—it's modifying the noun (or pronoun in this case).
Nouns and pronouns require an adjective.

But what if I said I feel fabric gently before buying it? In this case,
feel indicates a physical action, which makes it an action verb, which
calls for an adverb, *gently.*

The bottom line is that to use an adverb you need an action verb,
so look at your sentence and figure out if you're talking about an
action or a condition of being.

Nonparallelism

Non-what now? Parallelism is a grammar rule that states that when two or more items are combined by a coordinating conjunction, all items must be grammatically the same. I discuss this again in appendix B, and it's something I see a lot when I'm editing (or just reading *anything*).

They built a mall, a movie theater, and they added two stoplights.

This sentence has a compound direct object comprised of two nouns and a clause, and that's not right. In order for the sentence to be parallel, all three items in the list must be the same part of speech—in this case, all nouns. Here are a few options for fixing the sentence:

They built a mall, a movie theater, and two stoplights.
They built a mall and a movie theater, and they added two stoplights.
They built a mall and a movie theater. They also added two stoplights.

Can you spot the nonparallelism in the following sentences?
1. I counted four geese, two chickens, and I even saw a pig.
2. He was tall, he had deep blue eyes and dark hair.
3. Viewers found the movie funny, quirky, a roller-coaster ride, and original.

Here are the answers:
1. As in the example above, #1 has two nouns combined with a clause. Change to "I counted four geese, two chickens, and one pig."
2. In this one, "dark hair" doesn't go with the list, which is a list

of clauses, so the sentence winds up being a comma splice ("he was tall" + "he had deep blue eyes and dark hair"). Change to "He was tall with deep blue eyes and dark hair."

3. Here we have three adjectives and one noun ([a roller-coaster] ride). Change to "Viewers found the movie funny, quirky, and original and thought it was a real roller-coaster ride." (Or scrap the metaphor and use an appropriate adjective: "Viewers found the movie funny, quirky, exciting, and original."

Overuse of Present Participles

I'm ridiculously confident in saying that you do this. Most of us do, myself included.

If you recall from previous chapters, present participles are verbs with -ing added to the end: going, moving, looking. Present participles indicate a continuous action, meaning an action that took place over time (past tense) or is currently ongoing (present tense) or will be happening during a future time (future tense). This usage is often quite appropriate.

Here are a couple of examples of proper usage:

She was driving home when her tire blew.
They were already looking for a new house when the fire happened.

Here's a reminder of the boring grammar: Present participles create what is called the progressive tense, which can be in the past (was going), present (is going), or future (will be going). And we tend to use this tense even when simple past, present, or future is more appropriate.

In the first example above, she was in the process of driving when her tire blew. In the second example, they were in the process of looking for a house when the fire happened. Both indicate ongoing actions that were occurring at the time of a secondary event, so the progressive tense is appropriate. But consider these examples:

He was working at the restaurant last summer.
They were building a house at the lake before I met them.

What's wrong with these sentences? Neither of them requires a continuous action. In the first example, the work at the restaurant happened during a specific time period that is now over. In the second example, the main action was completed before the secondary action took place (unlike in the first examples, in which the main action was ongoing when the secondary action happened). These sentences should be written as follows:

He worked at the restaurant last summer.
They built a house at the lake before I met them.

In other words, progressive tense was used instead of the more accurate simple past tense. We make this mistake all the time, but why? My theory, at least in part, is that the progressive tense comes across as softer, less bold than simple past, present, or future. Consider the difference between "I think you're wrong" and "I'm thinking you're wrong." Does the second one seem less confrontational? Do you read it differently? I suspect you do. If you don't, try reading them out loud and see if you read them differently. My guess is that you read the one in progressive tense with some hesitation, a softening of the blow, if you will.

I think we do this when we're talking because we want to seem less confrontational when we say something the other person may not want to hear, and over time this usage has come to sound more and more correct in general and then naturally spread from verbal to written use. That's a total theory of mine. I can't back it up with research; it just makes sense to me.

So what is there to do about it? When you encounter present participles in your writing, ask yourself if the progressive tense is really necessary. Are you talking about a truly ongoing action or are you talking about an action that can be expressed in simple past, present, or future?

> I'm wondering if you're available tonight.
>
> or
>
> I wonder if you're available tonight.
>
> They were driving all night.
>
> or
>
> They drove all night.

It might surprise you how often you use progressive tense with present participles when all you really need is simple past, present, or future.

The Lost Art of the Paragraph

Have you ever given any thought to the paragraph—what it is and why we use it? Paragraphs don't exist just to break up the monotony of a page full of text. They serve an actual purpose, which is more concrete in nonfiction writing (think of the five-paragraph essay), but they serve a purpose—more than one, in fact—in fiction and narrative nonfiction as well.

The classic paragraph uses the Topic Sentence–Supporting Sentences–Conclusion model that you likely learned in high school or college for use in essays and term papers. That exact structure doesn't do you much good in narrative writing except as a demonstration of the purpose of a paragraph, which is to impart a single idea and then support that idea.

So how does that help you? Consider this example:

> She wasn't sure what to do next. The boat listed in the soft ripples of the lake, the water lapping gently against the sides. The wind had died down and was now blowing just enough to tousle her bangs instead of blowing her hair every which way. Still, she decided to keep her hat on. She wondered what Jason was doing now that she was gone.

Did that first sentence make you think the paragraph would be about the character's conundrum? Were you expecting to learn about her options and possibly roadblocks? But you didn't get those things, did you? No, you did not! This is a good example of a rambling paragraph, one that lacks focus and leads the reader down a winding and possibly confusing path.

Even though narrative writing does not adhere to strict rules, the basic structure of a paragraph still matters. Consider this rewrite of the example:

> She wasn't sure what to do next. Since she'd forgotten to refill the gas can, the engine was no longer an option. And the wind had died down too much for the sails to be of any use. Even if she had oars, the boat was way too big for her to move it manually. So she sat in the middle of the lake with no land in sight, stranded and wondering what Jason was doing now that she was gone. He certainly wouldn't be looking for her.

OK, now we're getting somewhere. The first sentence leads into the sentences that follow it and support it, and those sentences lead us into the next topic, seamlessly setting up a transition into the next paragraph. It all makes sense (well, it would in context) and is easy to follow.

Some things to keep in mind about paragraphs:

1. Paragraphs can be long or short, but either way, they should be focused. Paragraphs of more than a couple of sentences should take their cue from the first sentence as to what the focus should be.

2. Just like the story itself, each paragraph should have a natural flow to it—and this applies to moving from one paragraph to the next as well. Paragraphs that jump around from one topic to another can be confusing and tiresome to readers.

3. Transitions are very helpful to readers, so it's good to build in a natural transition at the end of one paragraph, as I did, or to use some sort of transition at the beginning of the next paragraph. The occasional jarring shift in topic/focus from one paragraph to the next is OK, but do it too often and readers might get annoyed.

4. Today's readers tend to shy away from long paragraphs, so keep that in mind as you go. Long paragraphs aren't forbidden, but it's best to not use too many, especially in a row.

5. Then again, don't go overboard with single-sentence or super short paragraphs, either, because they can make your writing choppy and awkward if overused.

Also keep in mind the triggers for when to switch to a new paragraph. According to MasterClass, "A paragraph break is necessary when starting a new topic, introducing a new speaker, contrasting other POVs or ideas, or providing white space to give readers a pause from a longer paragraph."[1]

That second one in the list is a big deal in narrative writing: "introducing a new speaker." In almost all instances (the exceptions are rare), you should not have two or more characters speaking in the same paragraph. It's very confusing for readers who are used to a certain structure.

Not this:

"I can't find my keys," Shannon said. She started pulling the cushions off the sofa while she grumbled to herself words I probably didn't want to hear. "Did you check the freezer?" I chuckled at this suggestion, but she stopped what she was doing and marched to the kitchen.

Who said, "Did you check the freezer?" Did you pick up that the narrator said it? You may have anticipated that because it's in line with what I'm explaining, but in another context, would you have known? It's not really clear. Either character could have said it. Even if it had been tagged with "I said," you're still putting two speakers in the same paragraph, which can throw readers off.

Do this instead:

"I can't find my keys," Shannon said. She started pulling the cushions off the sofa while she grumbled to herself words I probably didn't want to hear.

"Did you check the freezer?" I chuckled at this suggestion, but she stopped what she was doing and marched to the kitchen.

The key here is to make sure that your paragraphs are easy to follow, that they don't ramble, and that you insert appropriate paragraph breaks to keep things making sense for readers.

Pet Peeves

When I say the following are pet peeves, of course I mean that they are some of *my* pet peeves. However, if I do my job right, they will soon be among your pet peeves too. You're welcome.

Pet Peeve #1: Misspelling Elongated Syllables

Wowww!

I don't know about you, but when I read something like the above, it sounds something like this in my head: *wowa-wa-wa!*

When you're spelling out an elongated syllable, *please* repeat the letters that are *actually being elongated: wooow!* Or, if you'd rather, *wo-o-ow!*

Other examples:

Hellooooo! (not Helllllllo!)
Mo-o-o-o-om! (not Mommmm!)
Sweeeet! (not Sweettttt!)

Rarely do we elongate consonant sounds, but those words are out there. If you aren't sure which letters to repeat, say the word in its elongated form out loud. What sounds do you hold? Those are the ones to elongate in writing.

Now, how you actually spell these words is another issue, and there aren't really any rules where that's concerned. Using hyphens works really well to help readers understand what you're doing. If you're holding out a vowel sound that's made by two vowels, I recommend repeating only the one vowel that represents the sound being elongated (we-e-eird).

The bottom line is that you want to spell the elongated word in a way that best represents how it should be pronounced. So if you aren't sure, say the word out loud and then spell it based on how you said it.

Pet Peeve #2: "Safety Deposit Box"

I watch a lot of crime dramas, and every crime drama has at least one episode involving bank robbers breaking into safe deposit boxes. So I confront this pet peeve *a lot*.

Assuming you pronounce "deposit" with a long *e* sound, if you say "safe deposit" out loud, "safe de—" sounds a lot like "safety." I have to assume this is what led to people deciding to use the term *safety deposit box* instead of *safe deposit box*. But when you break it down grammatically, you can clearly see which version of the term is correct.

Consider rearranging the words:

Safe Deposit Box =
Box for Safe Deposits =
Safe Box for Deposits

Safety Deposit Box =
Box for Safety Deposits =
Safety Box for Deposits

Do I need to explain?

Oh, you know I'm going to.

This construction comes down to meaning, more so than to grammar. We're talking about a box. What kind of box? A box for depositing things into, a deposit-box, if you will. What kind of deposit-box is it? A safe one. Now obviously we don't spell it with a hyphen, but hopefully using the hyphen here gives you a clearer idea of what's happening. It's a safe "deposit-box," not a safety "deposit-box," which doesn't read well at all. (But if you want a grammatical explanation, remember that the first word has to modify the noun phrase "deposit box." *Safe* is an adjective. *Safety* is a noun. There you go.)

Pet Peeve #3: "A for Effort"

I'm sure there are some elementary schools out there that give grades to their kindergartners for effort, but that's not the origin of this phrase. For this phrase, effort is not the subject. *It's the grade.* So "A for Effort" literally means you're grading the student's grade. What?!

When I was in kindergarten, we were given these grades:

As you can see from the scan of my *actual* kindergarten report card, I was a pretty good student when I was five years old (and I could print my own name like a pro!). But more importantly, you can see how the grades *E, S,* and *I* were used (well, not *I* because I was an *S* or better right out of the gate, thank you very much!).

ACADEMIC GROWTH

	REPORT PERIOD					
	1	2	3	4	5	6
I can print my name	E	E	E	E		
I can tell a story in proper sequence	S	S	S	S		
I can relate my experience to the group	S	S	S	S		
I use complete sentences			S	S		
I see likenesses and differences in objects, pictures and letters	S	S	S	S		
I know how to handle a book correctly			S	S		
I can recall parts of stories		S	S+	S+		
I can recite short poems	E	E	E	E		
I can hear sounds of letters	S	S+	E	E		
I recognize letters	S	S+	E	E		
I can count objects	S	S	S	S		
I understand numbers	S	S	S	S		
I recognize numbers	S	S	S	S		
I know simple number vocabulary			S	S		
I know the colors	S	S	S	S		
I am curious and want to know more about my environment	S	S	S	S		

Now my school used Excellent, Satisfactory, and Improving, but many other schools used, and perhaps still use, a grading scale that included the grade of Effort, which was similar to my report card's use of Improving, meaning the student tries hard but still struggles. So again, *Effort is the grade,* not the subject.

So please don't say "A for Effort." The correct phrase is "E for Effort."

Pet Peeve #4: Saying Someone Was Hung to Death

As weird as it may seem, the word *hang* has two past tense forms. *Hung* is used in every situation except one: death by hanging. When referring to this circumstance, the correct form is *hanged.*

> He hung his coat on the hook.
> They hanged him by the neck.

Pet Peeve #5: Yeah, Yea, and Yay

Three oh-so-misused and -misunderstood little words. Let's compare:

Yay: a celebratory outcry; rhymes with *day*

Yea: a vote in the affirmative (opposite of *nay*); also rhymes with *day*

Yeah: a casual affirmative; pronounced similar to *yam*

> "Yay! The council voted yea on Prop 217!"
> "Yeah, that's amazing."

As an honorable mention, let's talk about the word *ya*, which isn't a word in English at all, not even slang. Some people use it as a colloquial spelling for *you*, but it is not any kind of spelling for *yes*, so please don't use it that way.

Pet Peeve #6: Referring to a Company as a Person

Regardless of what the US Supreme Court might say, a company is not a person. Consider the following:

> The People's Bank, who contributes millions every year to charities, insists they've never cheated on their taxes.

What's wrong here? First, a company is a *that*, not a *who*. Second, *they* and *their* refer to living entities, which a company is not. Additionally, *they* and *their* are plural, and a company is a singular unit (and treated as singular, grammatically, in American English). Now consider this:

> The People's Bank, which contributes millions every year to charities, insists it's never cheated on its taxes.

Now, perhaps you don't like how *it's* and *its* sound in this sentence. It might bug you to refer to an entity that is made up of people as an "it." If that's the case, then make sure you talk about the people behind the company, not the company itself:

> The executives of the People's Bank, who contribute millions every year to charities, insist they've never cheated on their taxes.

In this example, *who, they,* and *their* refer to the executives, not the company.

To be honest, not everyone agrees with me here. There are those who would say that referring to a company as a living being is just fine if you're ultimately referring to the people in the company, which you could argue is the case in my first example. But my opinion is that, unless you're talking in metaphor, people = *they* and company = *it.*

Pet Peeve #7: Misuse of *Literally*

The following definition for *literally* appears in *Merriam-Webster's* online dictionary:

> "in effect : VIRTUALLY—used in an exaggerated way to emphasize a statement or description that is not literally true or possible"[2]

In case that definition confuses you, what *M-W* is saying is that the term *literally* can be used to mean *virtually*, but in a sarcastic or satirical way. And I get it, but . . .

He was so mad, his head literally exploded.

Yuck.

You should not use this type of exaggeration unless it's in a character's voice—for example, in first-person narration or dialogue—and then only if it's the type of exaggeration that the character would use. But in all other situations—third-person narrator, characters who know how the English language works—avoid using *literally* to mean *virtually* because it literally drives me nuts (this is not an exaggeration!).

Pet Peeve #8: "On Accident"

You have my copy editor to thank for this one. She mentioned it to me, and now I'm passing it along to you so that we can all be annoyed by it. The correct prepositional phrase is "by accident," and there is no condition in which "on accident" is correct.

Chapter 9

Show, Don't Tell

If you've spent any time researching writing techniques, you've heard of *show, don't tell* (heck, I've already mentioned it several times). This mantra is tricky because it's both a very good idea and a very dangerous one.

The danger of *show, don't tell* comes from the likelihood of overuse, which can make reading a story akin to trudging through a dense bog. No one wants to read that story. No one wants to read a boring story either, so the art of *show, don't tell* is certainly one to cultivate.[1]

Consider the difference between taking a photograph and painting a picture. A photograph renders a nearly exact replica of the subject, whereas a painting is interpretive and unique (even a photo-realistic painting bears the mark of the artist). Yes, good photography requires skill, technique, and even artistry, just like painting. But here's the deal: Watching someone take a photo, while perhaps interesting, is not very exciting (for most people—no disrespect to the photographers out there). On the other hand, watching someone paint a picture is more captivating. It starts as nothing and transforms into something real right before your eyes. It's almost magical. And while you may prefer an Ansel Adams photo to a Bob Ross painting, I'm betting you'll agree that Bob Ross was way more fun to watch.

And a story that uses a healthy balance of *show, don't tell* is way more fun to read. So don't give your readers a photograph. Paint them a picture.

What Is Telling?

Telling is handing someone a photograph and saying, "This." It means simply to state something outright, whether that's an emotion, an action, a thought, or a description. Telling leaves little to the imagination and yet, somehow, also gives little information.

The trees were bare.

Without any context, this sentence could be telling us any number of things, but let's assume it means that the trees have no leaves. That's really all we know, since there are also many different reasons why a tree might lose its leaves. So while this sentence may bring to mind a vivid image of bare-branched trees, it gives us almost no other information.

Telling sentences aren't necessarily short like the one above. Let's add to it a little:

The trees were bare, and Sheila felt lonely as she watched them.

Longer, more information, but not much better. We now have Sheila staring at the bare trees and feeling lonely, but we still know almost nothing. What kind of trees are they? Why are they bare? Is it seasonal? Are they dead? If so, what killed them? And what's up with Sheila? Is she alone? Is she staring out a window? Why is she lonely? How is she behaving? What is her posture, her expression? How about some nonverbal cues?

When you leave so many questions unanswered, you're telling. When you answer the questions, you're showing.

Is Telling Always Bad?

Nope. Telling has its place, as does everything else the experts keep telling you not to do. There is value in telling. According to well-storied.com in their post "How to Balance 'Show, Don't Tell' in Your Writing," telling can serve the following functions:

+ Showing the passage of time
+ Relaying simple backstory or exposition
+ Capturing the narrative voice of a character
+ Expressing a simple statement
+ Crafting dialogue
+ Transitioning between settings
+ Balancing lengthy "showing" descriptions
+ Highlighting an important thought or action[2]

Let's explore a few of these through examples:

Twelve years later, Arnie found himself back in Paris surrounded by the family he thought he'd lost.

In this example, we have a lengthy passage of time, which we can assume is being skipped over because nothing relevant to the story happened during that time. We also have a change of setting in this sentence. Again, if nothing that occurred during the move to Paris has any bearing on the story, there's no need to go into details. Simply stating that it happened is sufficient.

She stood motionless, too stunned to move.

Short, simple statements like this one can have a lot of impact, especially when emotions are high or when you're creating suspense. Long-winded descriptions can suck the tension right out of the moment.

Silence engulfed the farm like the clouds that filled the sky and cast shadows across the snow-laden hills. The trees were bare. The creek trickled beneath its blanket of ice while the sun struggled to penetrate the cold of winter.

In this example, our boring little telling sentence, "The trees were bare," actually pops. It contrasts the heady description in the first and last sentences and creates an effective balance between showing and telling.

What Is Showing?

Showing is painting the picture. Showing means describing the *actions* of the setting, the character, and so on in order to allow readers to use their imaginations about what those actions mean. Showing means bringing your readers into the story and making them part of it. In the previous example, I could have just written, "It was winter and the sky was overcast," but there isn't anything engaging about that sentence. And the ultimate goal of showing is to engage your reader.

Telling

He became angry.

Showing

His face bore a crimson like a pile of rubies, and his body stiffened as his hands tightened into fists.

Telling

She hated to see him go.

Showing

She didn't try to hold back the tears as he turned the car and disappeared around the corner.

Telling

The trees were bare, and Sheila felt lonely as she watched them.

Showing

Sheila sulked with her elbows propped on her bedroom windowsill and her chin resting in her hands. She cocked her head to one side as the barren oak trees shivered in the subzero breeze. Her ears stung with the reverberations of music and laughter that wafted up from her parents' holiday party: no kids allowed.

The Dangers of Showing

The examples above indicate that showing over telling can be very effective; however, showing can also get seriously out of control.

Have you ever tried painting and worked so hard on one section that you added too much paint and ruined the image? *And we're back to the dangers of adjectives and adverbs.* While the right descriptors can enhance an image, too many descriptors will ruin it. Consider an embellished version of the Sheila example.

Original Sentence:
Sheila sulked with her elbows propped on her bedroom windowsill and her chin resting in her hands.

Embellished Sentence:
Sheila sulked with her tiny elbows propped unhappily on her narrow, dusty oak windowsill and her stubborn chin resting unsettled in her cupped five-year-old hands.

Now, you might think that's not so bad. But imagine an entire story written that way. Ugh! Limit the use of descriptors and consider which descriptions actually matter. Do we need to know that her windowsill is narrow or dusty or oak? Probably not, so leave it out. Stick to the relevant information and keep it simple.

Tips for Effective Showing

Bring Sensory Experiences to Life

Certain verbs indicate that a sensory experience is on the way: *heard, felt, saw, smelled,* and so on. These verbs tell us what the character is experiencing. She heard a wolf howl. OK, whatever. How about instead, the hairs on the back of her neck bristled as a wolf howled in the distance. I no longer have to tell you that she heard the howl, do I? Her physical reactions do the telling for me. There's also more action in the revised sentence, which makes it even more engaging.

When dealing with sensory experiences, don't just tell us that they happened. Describe the physical reactions to them and what triggered those reactions.

Be Mindful of "Thought" Verbs

Thought, considered, remembered, pondered, and the like—these verbs indicate that the author is about to tell us something. And that's not necessarily bad. Sometimes we really just need to know what a character is thinking. Sometimes, however, bringing those thoughts to life is more effective.

Telling

Andy thought about last year's chaotic road trip.

Showing

A vision of the flat tires, lost luggage, and seedy motel rooms from last year's road trip flashed through Andy's mind.

Notice I'm still telling you what he was thinking, but I'm describing it in specific terms so you can see in your mind what he sees in his mind.

Avoid Adjectives Indicating Emotions

Happy, sad, jealous, angry, bored—these adjectives don't paint much of a picture. Besides, your readers are savvy enough to figure out how your characters feel based on your descriptions of their actions and reactions to stimuli.

Telling

Tina was very excited to win the contest.

Showing

Tina jumped in the air and squealed, a smile overtaking her face and igniting her eyes.

Describe Nonverbal Indicators

We're talking body language and vocal cues here: posture, gestures, facial expressions, tone of voice, what have you. Nonverbal communication comprises two-thirds or more of all communications, so don't ignore this aspect of your characters' actions, reactions, and interactions.

Consider how much we learn from the nonverbal descriptions in the example from the previous section: Tina jumped in the air and squealed, a smile overtaking her face and igniting her eyes. We know that Tina is excited and happy, just from these nonverbal cues.

Replace Adverbs and Adjectives with Strong Nouns and Verbs

As we've already discussed, adjectives and adverbs can mask weak nouns and verbs. Again, look to the previous example. I could have said, Tina jumped in the air and squealed with a giant smile and bright, shiny eyes. But there isn't a whole lot of excitement in that description. Instead, we have her smile overtaking her face and igniting her eyes. Same basic description, but so much more emotion and not an adjective or adverb in sight.

Telling

He ran frantically into the empty, desolate warehouse.

Showing

He scrambled into the warehouse, which greeted him with nothing but cobwebs and the echoes of his own heartbeat.

There isn't a single descriptor in that sentence, yet the image is clear. (Yes, *own* is an adjective, but not a descriptive one.)

Use Targeted Language

Try to avoid using generic terms or, in lieu of that, mix in specific information to give those generic terms context. In the example below, *fed* and *dog* are nonspecific terms that leave us with questions. (How was the dog fed? What type of dog is it?) Our rewrite using specific terms answers these questions.

Telling

Joe fed his hungry dog.

Showing

While Joe filled Buddy's dish with kibble, the dog barked and bounced and smiled its puggish smile.

We now know not only what Joe did (fed his dog) but also how he did it (filled the dish with kibble), and we know the type of dog (pug, indicated by its "puggish smile"). In addition, we've replaced the adjective *hungry* by describing the dog's reaction (barking, bouncing, smiling) to being fed. Now we don't just know what happened. We can see it.

Show Through Dialogue

Telling

Joe refused to participate in the hazing because he didn't want anyone to get hurt.

Showing

"I won't do it, Mark," Joe insisted. "Someone could get hurt, and I won't be a part of it."

Dialogue can serve just about every aspect of a story, from developing plot and character to creating a sense of place to building backstory. You can tell a full, rich story with nothing but dialogue.

That's how powerful it is, whether it's a conversation between two or more characters, a character talking to themselves, or inner dialogue. This is one of the greatest tools you have as a writer, so use it well.

Also note that when a *narrator* says something, it's telling. But when a *character* says it, it's showing:

Telling

She decided to give the money back.

Showing

"I've thought long and hard about it, and I'm definitely going to give the money back."

(However, beware the dreaded info dump. Characters should tell through dialogue only when it's natural and suits the situation.)

Show, Don't Tell Versus the Narrator's Voice

Let's assume you don't really want your book to sound like it was written by Tolstoy. Perhaps you want your narrator to have a more conversational tone or your narrator is one of your characters. You might be thinking that the examples in this chapter sound a bit generic, and you're wondering how to accomplish the things suggested here while still maintaining your narrator's voice.

Yeah, that's a valid concern. The good news is twofold:

1. It's totally possible to show in a conversational tone or to do so in a specific character's voice. You "simply" (she said through an evil laugh) have to figure out how your narrator would do it. Consider the differences between the following two examples:

> Pamela smiled, but when she raised her eyebrow, I froze.
> When Pamela smiled and raised one eyebrow, Jack Nicholson's Joker flashed through my mind.

Same message in both examples and some similar wording, but only a specific type of narrator would use the second example. So showing is adaptable, and it doesn't have to sound generic or like high-minded literary fiction.

2. When writing in first person, it's totally OK to tell instead of show if it fits your character/narrator's personality. Still try to work in showing wherever it makes sense to do so in order to bring your readers deeper into the story, but only do so when it suits the narrator. A consistent narrator voice is more important.

It's All About Triggering Your Readers' Imaginations

Another way to think about showing versus telling is that showing is a book while telling is a movie. Lots of people prefer reading books because they get the chance to use their imaginations, to picture the characters and settings and action for themselves. That's not possible with a movie. When I watch *Mission: Impossible*, Tom Cruise looks the way he looks. I can't choose to picture him looking different (why would I?) because he's *right there*. But if I were reading a book about that character, I could picture that character any way I wanted (probably like Tom Cruise!).

Showing stimulates your readers' imaginations and allows them to picture your characters, your settings, your action, and so on in ways that make sense to *them* (book) instead of telling them everything and effectively spoon-feeding them and forcing them to see everything your way (movie).

When you describe a character's physical reaction to something, you show us how they feel and what they think. When you describe what the weather is doing, you give us a sense of setting. When you describe the movement of the trees or the behavior of animals, you give us a sense of place and atmosphere.

Showing is about putting the reader in the moment by creating a tangible, living, breathing world. And while you must be careful not to overdo it, the right balance of showing and telling will create an engaging narrative that your readers won't want to put down.

Practice *Show, Don't Tell*

Rewrite the following sentences to make them more descriptive. Use interesting nouns and verbs, keep adjectives to a minimum, and avoid adverbs. Use your imagination! See my rewrites on page 229.

NOTE: Don't just elaborate on these sentences. *Replace* them.

Example:
Getting the new house made Ariana so happy.

Rewrite:
After getting the news about the house, Ariana danced through the kitchen, singing "All I Do Is Win," and spent the rest of the day smiling.

1. The city is beautiful at night.

2. She felt bad about not showing up to the party.

3. Everyone thought he was unusual.

4. It was a cold and wintery day.

5. Omar waited impatiently for five o'clock to arrive.

6. Trevor didn't understand the instructions.

7. They always arrive late.

8. It was the car of his dreams and he wished he could afford it.

9. Amelia tried not to cry when she broke her ankle.

10. There was nothing Carl could do but wait.

Chapter 10

Perspective Versus Point of View

If you're like me, you get these concepts mixed up all the time. While they are interrelated and very similar, they are also distinct. So why are they so easy to confuse?

I would say it's all a matter of perspective, but I fear you would hold that against me. Let's just say it depends on your point of view.

When I first started learning about perspective and point of view *from a literary standpoint*, I found them very confusing, perspective in particular. I found it difficult—and still do—to refer to one term without using the other term as a synonym. The problem is that, for certain definitions, point of view and perspective *are* synonyms. However, in a literary sense, they are quite different. Point of view is directly connected to the narrator, while perspective relates to the characters.

Point of view (POV) tells us who the narrator is, what the narrator knows, and, to some degree, how the narrator will tell the story. Perspective tells us how the characters view the events unfolding around them and how those perceptions influence who they are and why they do what they do.

Perspective

The following definition is taken from the *NY Book Editors* blog post "What's the Difference Between Perspective and Point of View?"

"Perspective is how the characters view and process what's happening within the story."[1]

Basically, perspective is how we interpret the world around us. Perspective is unique to each individual. This is why five witnesses can tell five very different versions of the same event. Each person has their own way of interpreting what they saw, and each interpretation affects how they remember what they saw. Their perspectives vary, so their stories vary.

Take a young woman born and raised in rural Iowa and an elderly Chilean man visiting the US for the first time, and put them side by side on a flight. Then ask them to describe the experience. Chances are you will get two vastly different descriptions. The life experiences, beliefs, culture, age, gender, and so on of each person will influence how they interpret the people and events around them.

That's perspective. No perspective is better or worse than another. Just different.

Origins of Perspective

A character's perspective is influenced by the following (and more):

+ Where they're from
+ How they were / are being raised
+ What they believe
+ How they identify
+ Whom they spend time with
+ How much education they have
+ How easily influenced they are
+ What their dreams and goals are
+ What their fears are

In order to fully understand a character's perspective, you, as author, must understand the character's backstory, beliefs, goals, influences, and fears. You must know these things—*even if you don't share them with your readers*—because these are the details that will help you build and shape full, believable, and *consistent* characters.

Respecting Your Characters' Perspectives

Keep in mind that *there is no such thing as an invalid perspective.* Even when we're talking about villains, those villains have a perspective that's valid—to them.

I don't want to assume that you've read/seen Harry Potter, but I'm going to assume that you've read/seen Harry Potter. Consider the character Snape, whose perspective (the true nature of which is unknown to readers until the end) influences everything he does. We may not understand it or agree with it, but it's totally valid *to him*. And we may not agree with or like the things he does, but those things align with his perspective, making them valid actions *to him*.

All this means that, in order for you to create great characters, you have to accept each character's perspective as being valid. You don't have to like them or agree with them. But if you don't accept their perspectives, you'll have a difficult time making them fully formed, interesting characters whom readers can connect with, care about, or at the very least, be curious about. Why? Because how can you create believable characters if you don't believe in them yourself? That all starts with understanding and accepting their perspectives.

Point of View

The concept of POV can be confusing because *people* have a point of view and *stories* have a point of view—and they aren't the same thing! A character's point of view is the same as their perspective. A story's point of view—which is all about the narrator—is what we're going to talk about here. This is what we mean when we talk about *literary* point of view.

Before you start writing a story, you have to decide who is going to tell it. In other words, **who** is your narrator? Is it one of your characters or an unknown entity? And **how much** does your narrator know? Is the narrator omniscient or limited to the knowledge of one or more specific characters? Finally, you must know **how** the narrator will tell the story.

Who

The narrator can be the main character in the story, a character who is present but not actually part of the story (someone who watches what's happening but doesn't participate), an unknown entity, or pretty much anyone or anything else. The narrator could be an animal or a piece of furniture, if you're inclined to anthropomorphism.

You can even have multiple narrators, which isn't easy but plenty of authors have done it. And, of course, the narrator could be you. Regardless of who you choose to tell the story, you must make this decision first.

How Much

Next you need to decide how much your narrator knows. Does the narrator know absolutely everything about everything (the omniscient narrator)? Does the narrator know only what they personally experience (as a character in the story)? Or does the narrator know about the experiences of multiple characters but not all of them?

How

How will the narrator tell the story? As an observer or as a participant?

Three Points of View

There are three basic points of view: first person, second person, and third person. First and third person also break down into multiple subtypes. Let's take a look.

First Person

Who: A character in the story
How Much: They know only what they personally hear or experience.
How: They can be a participant in or an observer of the story.

First-person POV is characterized by the use of the personal pronouns *I, me,* and *we.* A character within the story tells it from their own perspective. They may or may not, however, be the protagonist. A secondary character can just as easily tell the story (think *The Great Gatsby*).

The first-person narrator can give the reader only that information that the narrator personally experiences, either through direct experience or through hearsay.

For example, let's say we have a story about Jane and Tarzan. If Jane is the first-person narrator, she cannot tell us what Tarzan is doing when they aren't together. There's no way for Jane to know that. She can speculate, but she cannot give us information about him that she didn't personally witness or hear about from someone else (and if she did hear it from someone else, she should tell us that).

These are the types of first-person narrator:

The Protagonist: The main character tells their own story.

Secondary Character: A character just to the left of center tells the story. This character is more than just a casual observer. They actually take part in the story. Again, think *The Great Gatsby.* Nick Carraway, the narrator, is a secondary character. Gatsby is the protagonist.

Peripheral Character: A character who observes the story but has little to no involvement with it. A great example here is *The*

Book Thief, told by Death, who is merely a casual observer of the story and does not interact with the characters.

Unreliable Narrator: Any of the three narrators listed could be an unreliable narrator, meaning they cannot be trusted because of their own flaws or ulterior motives. Unreliable narrators include children (through lack of experience and naïveté), con artists (who are out to help only themselves), characters with mental illness (through a warped sense of reality), and braggarts (who exaggerate their own importance or worth).

You could have a second- or third-person unreliable narrator, but that might get too confusing for the reader, especially when the narrator is an unknown entity. Most unreliable narrators are first-person narrators.

Second Person

Who: An unknown entity or a peripheral character
How Much: They know only as much as the protagonist knows.
How: Varies

Second-person POV is characterized by use of the pronouns *you* and *your*. I'm not talking about the narrator simply addressing the reader. In second-person point of view, the reader actually becomes the protagonist. Most second-person POV books have an unknown entity as the narrator, but the narrator could also be a known entity, like a peripheral character or even the author.

There are more books out there that use second-person POV than you might think. For an amusing example, check out Neil Patrick Harris's *Choose Your Own Autobiography,* in which Harris casts the reader as himself and the reader gets to choose how the story progresses.

Here's the first sentence of Harris's book: "You, Neil Patrick Harris, are born in Albuquerque, New Mexico, on June 15, 1973, at what you're pretty sure is St. Joseph's Hospital, although it's hard to be certain as the whole experience leaves you a little blurry."[2]

To further understand how second-person narration works, let's do a comparison using a much less amusing, random passage from Ernest Hemingway's *A Farewell to Arms*, which is written in first person:

> Before I put on my coat I cut the cloth stars off my sleeves and put them in the inside pocket with my money. My money was wet but was all right. I counted it. There were three thousand and some lire. My clothes felt wet and clammy and I slapped my arms to keep the circulation going.[3]

Now I'll do the unthinkable and change Mr. Hemingway's text, in this case, to second person. I've also shifted it to present tense because I think second-person POV is most effective in the present.

> Before you put on your coat you cut the cloth stars off your sleeves and put them in the inside pocket with your money. Your money is wet but is all right. You count it. There are three thousand and some lire. Your clothes feel wet and clammy and you slap your arms to keep the circulation going.

And there you go, as weird as it may seem. Second-person point of view is unusual, and it could turn off some readers if they can't get into the experience of being the protagonist in a story. But that doesn't mean you shouldn't try it if you feel like it. I suspect that, if you do, your readers will remember the experience!

Third Person

Who: *An unknown entity*
How Much: *Varies*
How: *Strictly as an observer*

In third person, we see the use of third-person pronouns like *he, she, it,* and *they* and no use of *I, me,* or *we.* In third person, the narrator is strictly an unknown observer recounting the story and has no personal interaction with the story at all. The fact that the narrator is unknown is a key characteristic here because if the narrator were known to us, they'd be a character and we'd be in first person.

There are three types of third-person narrator:

Third-person limited tells the story from a single character's perspective. This POV is similar to first person in that the narrator knows only what that one character (usually the protagonist) knows. For example, in our story about Jane and Tarzan, I can use third-person limited to tell the story from Jane's perspective and, just like in that first-person example, the narrator can know only what Jane knows.

Third-person multiple tells the story from more than one character's perspective. In the first edition of this book, I mistakenly said that the perspective can change chapter by chapter, but that was wrong. If you switch the perspective chapter by chapter, you're still using third-person *limited* because you're still in only one character's head *at a time.* For example, say you have three best friends as protagonists and you switch perspective from one to another chapter by chapter—in other words, you get into the head and share the thoughts and feelings and direct experiences of only one friend per chapter. This is third-person limited. However, if the narrator knows and intermingles the thoughts and feelings and direct experiences of all three friends, *that's* third-person multiple.

In third-person multiple, the narrator knows everything the POV characters know (POV characters are the characters whose perspective the story is being told through), but the narrator's knowledge is still limited to just those POV characters, no one else. For example, the narrator might know everything about both Jane and Tarzan but nothing (except what Jane and Tarzan know) about the other characters.

Third-person omniscient tells the story from an all-knowing perspective. An omniscient narrator knows everything about everyone. They can tell us whatever they want about Jane or Tarzan or Clayton or Kala or anyone else in the story. There are no secrets from this narrator, and the only question for the author is how much of that knowledge they want to share.

Honorable mention: Some people have identified another type of third-person narration, known as **deep third**, which is just another way of saying deep POV. I don't use this category, and you'll see why when you read the deep POV chapter (chapter 11).

Mixed Points of View

Some novels use a mixture of points of view, which can get tricky and confusing, and the last thing you want is confused readers. Confused readers are unhappy readers who give very bad reviews. Use caution when mixing POVs. There's no reason you can't do it, as long as you do it well.

A great example of mixed points of view is Fannie Flagg's *Fried Green Tomatoes at the Whistle Stop Cafe*, in which Flagg uses no fewer than three different POVs:

+ **First person:** The *Weems Weekly* chapters, which are "reprints" of the fictional weekly bulletin from Whistle Stop, Alabama, are written by Dot Weems from her own perspective. These chapters are set in the 1930s.
+ **Third-person omniscient:** In many of the other 1930s chapters, Flagg uses an omniscient narrator to tell the story of Idgie, Ruth, and others.
+ **Third-person limited:** Then again, some of the 1930s chapters focus on a single character and use third-person limited POV in recounting those characters' experiences.
+ **Third-person limited plus first person:** The 1980s chapters are told through third-person limited, from Evelyn's point of view; however, Flagg also uses dialogue to work in a lot of first-person narration through the lengthy stories recounted by Ninny.

To keep the times and places straight, Flagg begins each chapter with a location and a date, without which the book would be very hard to follow. The result is an easy-to-navigate story told by multiple narrators from multiple points of view and perspectives.

Perspective Through Point of View

Let's look at how perspective and point of view work together.

Take *The Great Gatsby* for a moment. Nick Carraway is the narrator who is both sympathetic toward and in awe of Jay Gatsby. Therefore, he tells the story of his time with Gatsby with reverence and compassion. Nick Carraway's perspective sets the tone for the novel.

But what if Carraway had viewed Gatsby with contempt, distrust, or dislike? I imagine it would have been a much different story in which Carraway would have painted Gatsby as someone who deserved his fate, as opposed to being a victim of circumstance and bad luck.

Change the POV character's perspective (and in this case, the narrator's), and you change the whole story.

Regardless of the chosen POV, the perspective from which the story is written influences the tone of the story, the information the narrator chooses to share, and the way the reader responds to the characters.

First-person perspective is pretty easy because the narrator is one of the characters telling the story from their own perspective. Once you nail down the personal details of that character, you have a solid foundation for their perspective.

In second and third person, it's not the narrator's perspective that matters. It's the perspective of the POV character or characters.

Using our previous example, in third-person limited, it's a single character's (Jane's) perspective that influences the telling of the story (this would be the case in second person as well). In third-person multiple, it's both Jane's and Tarzan's perspectives that matter. In third-person omniscient, any and all characters' perspectives can influence the story.

To Sum It Up

When we're talking about literary perspective, we're talking about how the characters view and interpret the world around them. Each character has a unique perspective, which will influence how those characters behave within the story.

When we're talking about point of view, we're talking about the narrator—who is telling the story and how. Point of view can be in first person, second person, or third person. In first person, one of the characters tells the story from their own perspective. In second person, an unknown entity, a secondary character, or the author tells the story from the reader's (as protagonist) perspective. In third person, an unknown entity tells the story through the eyes of one or more characters or through omniscience.

Once you've mastered these concepts, you'll only be left with remembering not to use the terms interchangeably, which may be the hardest part about it. Good luck!

Practice Point of View

Write a short story from three different points of view. Think flash fiction here. You don't want to be writing multiple versions of a 5,000-word story (or maybe you do). See my stories on page 232.

Story: A young couple faces the challenges of planning a wedding.
Points of view:

First person: One of the characters tells the story from their own perspective.

Third-person limited: Tell the story in third person from the *other* character's perspective.

Third-person omniscient: Tell the story using both characters' perspectives at the same time.

HINT: To make this exercise appropriately challenging, write the exact same story three different ways. This will force you to rethink the perspective of each version and further your understanding of the differences. For example, consider the differences between "I couldn't help but laugh at George's ridiculous faux pas" and "George couldn't believe that Henry would laugh at his understandable mistake." In the first sentence, we see Henry's take on the situation. In the second, we get George's perspective. See if you can repeat this type of rewriting as you take on this exercise.

Chapter 11

What the Heck Is Deep POV?

Deep POV is a strategy for creating immersive storytelling that has your readers burying their noses in your book and reading until two in the morning because they can't put it down.

But deep POV is tricky and can be very confusing—and hard. Just understanding what it's all about is hard, so take your time here. It's worth it.

Deep POV (point of view) can be very confusing for a number of reasons, not the least of which is that it's difficult to categorize. Is it actually a point of view? Maybe it's more about *character* point of view than *narrator* POV? Maybe it's both?

I've really struggled with how to define deep POV, and then I discovered the blog *Writers in the Storm* and, more specifically, the post "Embracing the Mystery: Deep POV" by guest blogger Lori Brown. There's a lot going on in this post, but basically Brown describes her own struggles with understanding deep POV and her conclusions about it. This is the part that blew my mind:

> I am no longer even sure that Deep POV is best described *as* a POV.
>
> I am increasingly convinced that Deep POV is more a state of mind. Multiple devices can bring readers closer to what a character is thinking, feeling, experiencing, and thus bring the reader deeper into the story—at a level that you, the author, can manipulate with increasing skill as you use it. You can bring the reader *only as far into the story as you want them to be*, at any point in your story, as it serves your purpose.[1]

Two things caught my attention here. First, perhaps deep POV doesn't count as an actual POV. Maybe deep POV is a little bit more (did I just turn into Dr. Seuss?). Deep POV uses literary devices and strategies to take a regular POV (third-person limited—see "Deep POV's POV") and create something new out of it. But the thing is, you're still in third-person limited—you're just in a refined version of it. So perhaps, indeed, deep POV is not a point of view in its own right. This helps me because trying to define deep POV as a whole separate point of view just has never made sense to me.

The second thing from Brown's blog post that resonates with me is the malleability of deep POV. I'm going to share with you several ways to create deep POV, but guess what? You don't have to use them all. And even if you do use them all, you don't have to be perfect about it. For example, I've struggled to find an example of a published book that meets *all* the criteria described in this chapter, and I keep finding "errors" (usually in the form of dialogue tags) and thinking, "Nope, not that one." But I'm being too strict. You can write in deep POV without using every single technique described in this chapter. Maybe you'll limit dialogue tags but not do away with them completely. Maybe you'll latch onto a couple of the tricks described and really master those but not mess with a couple of others that you don't care for.

The point here is that deep POV is really what you make of it and that any level at which you use these methods is going to help give your readers a more immersive experience. And that's the *ultimate* point here, after all.

My recommendation is that you try everything described in this chapter—really try to incorporate all of them in your efforts at deep POV—and as you become more comfortable with them, you can decide which of them resonate with you and which of them don't, which you want to use fully and which you want to just pepper into your deep POV. I'll let you know the truly critical steps, and you can decide for yourself on everything else.

And with that said . . .

What Is Deep POV?

OK, so it's a way to make the narration as immersive as possible, but what does that mean? A simple definition of deep POV is that it removes the narrator's voice and places readers inside the POV character's head as much as possible, allowing readers to experience the story as the POV character experiences it. (As a reminder, the POV character is the one whose perspective the story is being told through at any given time. The POV character can change as the story progresses.)

Yes, that's the *simple* definition. And that's really all I'm going to give you at this point because I can explain this thing a hundred different ways and still leave you not quite understanding what deep POV is all about. The best way to understand what it is, is to understand how to create it. So bear with me and keep reading. The "what" will become clearer and clearer as you learn more and more about the "how."

An Example of Deep POV

Before we go any further, let me give you an example of deep POV so you can have some idea of what the heck I'm even talking about.

First an example of "normal" narration:

John walked into the room. He stopped suddenly and felt a chill overtake him. He couldn't believe what he was seeing. How could Madeline be here?

"But I shot you. I buried you," he said.

Yet here she was, sitting at the dining room table and sipping from a glass of red wine, clean, calm, and even a bit seductive, with John's revolver resting in her lap.

And here it is in deep POV:

John walked into the room and stopped. He shuddered and the shaking radiated to his fingertips.

What? How can she . . . ?

"But I shot you. I buried you."

Madeline sat at the dining room table. She raised a glass of red wine in John's direction and rested back in her chair as she looked up at him, her chin down and a smile tugging at one side of her mouth.

This doesn't make sense. Wait. Is that my gun?

What's the Difference?

Let's look at some of the differences. First, we've added inner dialogue so that John can tell us how shocked he is instead of the narrator doing it. Are you curious why these thoughts aren't in italics? Explanation to come. The descriptors for how Madeline is sitting and what she's doing have been replaced with actions—so we're now showing what she looks like instead of just describing it. Also, the narrator doesn't reveal the existence of the gun—John does, and readers discover it at the same time he does.

These are just some of the elements that differentiate the second version from the first. Does the second version feel more immersive to you? Do you feel more inside the action and inside John's head? If I did my job as author correctly, you should. That's the power of deep POV.

Deep POV's POV

As I mentioned in the chapter introduction, deep POV uses third-person narration, but what I didn't say in the intro is that deep POV exists *only* in third-person point of view. Some say it can be used in first person, but that's just a lie. Ha! No, that's harsh. Let's call it a *mistake*. While you can use many of the techniques of deep POV in first-person narration, you aren't really *in* deep POV.

Why? Because the whole point of deep POV is to remove the narrator's voice, and you can't do that if your narrator is a character in the story. And why would you? That would just be weird. *I want my protagonist to tell the story but I want to silence her voice.* What?

No, no, that won't do. Use these techniques in first person as much as makes sense and is effective, but be aware that only an unknown entity—a third person—can be silenced in the way required for deep POV.

Another essential aspect of deep POV's POV is that third-person deep POV must be *limited,* as in limited to the perspective of *only one* character. Using deep POV with an omniscient narrator would be a nightmare, and even third-person multiple would be very confusing. Deep POV is difficult enough with a limited narrator, so don't overcomplicate it—stick to one POV character *at a time.*

This is a standard rule any time you're writing in third-person limited, but it's even more important in deep POV because without the narrator stepping in to keep things straight for readers, confusion can set in very quickly. You have to be extremely cautious in deep POV, and that means *third-person limited*—no exceptions!

As I mentioned in the previous chapter, some people have identified "deep third" as a subtype of third-person narration specific to deep POV. I don't use this term because it's shorthand for deep POV in third-person limited, and I prefer to use the actual names so that there's no confusion. Maybe it's the teacher in me—I like things to be very clear. If you encounter the term *deep third,* just know that it means deep POV using third-person limited narration.

Characteristics of Deep POV

In deep POV, you aren't just trying to make the story more accessible to your readers. You're trying to put them *inside* the story. They aren't casual observers of the story, and they aren't even walking along with the POV character. Readers are actually inside the POV character's mind, seeing the story unfold through that character's eyes. The following characteristics are how you get there.

1. **Use of *show, don't tell*.** In deep POV, showing is paramount because telling is done in the narrator's voice and, in deep POV, the narrator is silent. Also, many of the strategies for creating deep POV are also strategies for showing, as you'll see. So one of the best things you can do to learn deep POV is to master showing first.

2. **Little to no use of narration to explain or describe.** OK, this is a tricky one, because isn't this what narration is for? Yes, indeed. It's the narrator's job to explain the POV character's motivations and feelings and to describe settings and characters and so forth. But how do you do that when you've put a gag order on your narrator? You use actions, dialogue, and thoughts. In deep POV, the job of the narration is to get readers from point A to point B, to give readers information about what the characters and the world around them are *doing*. It's up to the readers to take that information—along with the dialogue and the POV character's thoughts—and interpret what all those things mean.

   Normal:

   Carolyn turned down the music so she could think. She hadn't expected her brother to just give her their grandparents' house, especially after it had been sitting vacant for so many years. She felt her heartbeat quicken at the thought of how run-down the place must be by now.

Deep POV:

Carolyn turned down the music.

Shh, shh. Think, think. I can't believe Gary gave me the house.

Her heartbeat quickened.

What's it been? Twenty-plus years since Grandma died? The place must be a run-down mess.

The Effect:

Notice how little narration there is in the deep POV version and that the narration describes actions only. In deep POV, that's the narrator's job. Even going back to our earlier example of deep POV with John and Madeline, notice that the narrator describes Madeline according to her physical characteristics only—how she's sitting, how her head is positioned, that she's just barely smiling, that she's raising her glass. In neither of these two examples does the narrator *explain* anything. The POV characters do it.

3. **Everything is presented from the POV character's perspective.** When a third-person narrator describes something, it's usually pretty generic. The narrator is simply trying to set the scene for the reader. However, when the POV character describes something, they do so from their personal perspective, and their descriptions are thus colored by their experiences, opinions, beliefs, and everything else that contributes to who they are. In deep POV, the narrator describes things

in the POV character's voice and, therefore, from that character's perspective. This is an extremely important aspect of deep POV—nothing should be described in generic terms. Everything should reflect the POV character's perspective.

Normal:

The paint hung off the neglected siding in large chunks, and several windows were broken. The front porch sagged on one side and the steps creaked and moaned with each footfall.

Deep POV:

Chunks of paint waved to Carolyn. Her hair blew into her face, and she tucked it behind her ear.

"Hello, peeling paint . . . and broken windows . . . and sagging porch." She scowled. "It's not like I blame you for your own disrepair, but I feel like you could have tried harder."

She walked up the steps, which greeted her every footfall. "Yeah, hi to you too. I know how you feel."

The Effect:

Instead of simply describing the scene, deep POV infuses the description with the character's thoughts and interpretations, which makes the scene more relatable for the readers. For example, instead of the paint just hanging there, we have it waving at Carolyn, which we know comes from her interpretation because she greets the paint back. This is an indication that we're in Carolyn's head and not just getting a showy description from the narrator.

Also notice that there's no mention of the wind blowing. Instead, we describe the effects the wind is having—the paint waving, Carolyn's hair blowing into her face. This is a further example of point #2. The narrator doesn't explain how the paint is waving but rather shows readers that the wind is blowing, thus leaving readers to sort out for themselves what's happening with the paint and further triggering their imaginations.

4. **Reader access to information is limited.** In third-person limited, the narrator can know only what the POV character knows and, thus, can share only that much information with the reader. However, third-person limited narrators break this rule—to some degree—all the time. They will often give descriptions and build scenes in such a way that reveals more than the POV character is already familiar with. In deep POV, that cannot happen. Readers should never find out anything before the POV character does.

Normal:

After twenty years of neglect, the house had become home to critters of all types, including a particularly friendly opossum. When Carolyn stepped up to the dilapidated house, she had no idea what awaited her inside.

Deep POV:

Carolyn reached for the doorknob. The smell of animal waste awoke her gag reflex, and she covered her mouth and nose with her hands.

Oh god, that's disgusting! What the hell is living in here?

She stepped into the house and pulled her shirt up over her mouth and nose.

"Thanks for the"—cough!—"house, Gary!"

She walked through the entryway, down the hall, and into the kitchen. An opossum lay on the counter with its tummy pointed to the ceiling. When their eyes met, the opossum sat up and leaned toward Carolyn, sniffing the air around her.

"No effin' way!" She ran out of the house and dove back into her car.

The Effect:

In the "normal" example, the narrator gives the readers foreknowledge about the opossum, stripping the readers of any chance at being surprised by it. By revealing everything to readers at the same time that the POV character experiences them, readers live the story in real time and have the opportunity to really feel what the character is feeling. Foreknowledge ruins this opportunity because the reader knows what's coming, leaving them to merely watch the character's reactions, not *feel* them.

Techniques for Deep POV

OK, those are all good ideas, but how do you accomplish them? Here are some of the more technical tricks for accomplishing deep POV.

1   **Use internal dialogue.** Internal dialogue (i.e., inner thoughts) is a cornerstone of deep POV, and you can't create deep POV without it (unless you want your POV character talking aloud to themselves *a lot*). Internal dialogue puts the readers in the POV character's head and makes the narrative more personal and intimate. This can help pull readers in and keep them riveted.

      NOTE: I'm sure you've already noticed that the internal dialogue I've used so far has not been in italics the way we would normally do it. I originally used italics for my deep POV inner thoughts and recommended it that way; however, I've since learned that italics are actually a way for the narrator to sneak in and tell readers what's going on: "*Hey, readers, this is an inner thought—see the italics?*" So in deep POV, internal dialogue should be roman (i.e., normal typeface). In most cases, readers won't have any trouble understanding what's happening. If you're concerned about it, then try always putting inner thoughts in their own paragraph, but don't do any special formatting beyond that.

Normal:

Carolyn sat in her car and watched two animal control workers bring out carriers with little critters in them—a total of five so far. She shuddered at the thought of all those animals living in her grandparents' house.

She stuck her head up through the sunroof. "You're not gonna kill them, right?"

"No, ma'am. We'll release them back into the wild."

Carolyn nodded and sank back into the car, knowing she had to get the house fixed up or those critters would all be back in no time.

Deep POV:

Carolyn sat in her car as two animal control workers brought pet carriers out of the house.

Four . . . Five . . . Gawd, how many animals were living in there anyway? Yuck.

She stuck her head up through the sunroof. "You're not gonna kill them, right?"

"No, ma'am. We'll release them back into the wild."

Carolyn nodded and sank back into the car.

I need to get a contractor out here. Those little critters ain't gonna stay gone long.

The Effect:

With internal dialogue, readers learn what they need to know by being inside the character's head and, through the character's thoughts, feeling what the character is feeling. This method is more interactive, more immersive, and perhaps most importantly, more interesting.

Keep in Mind:

When using inner dialogue to give information, it's very easy to use info dumps and to write the thoughts more like narration. The challenge is to give the information using words a person would actually think. For example, what sounds more natural? I think I'll follow him and see what he's doing **or** What is he up to? Maybe I should follow him . . . Yeah, that's happening.

2. **Avoid dialogue tags.** *He said, she replied, he answered, she asked,* and so on. These tags are not just minimized; they're removed entirely. Why? Well, ever heard of "the fourth wall"? It's a concept taken from theater and the idea that the audience is watching the action through an invisible fourth wall. If one or more of the actors addresses the audience directly, it's called "breaking the fourth wall." The same concept exists in TV, movies (ever seen *Ferris Bueller's Day Off?*), and even books. Dialogue tags are a way for the narrator to tell the reader who is speaking, which effectively breaks the literary fourth wall. It makes the reader aware of the narrator's presence, which is something deep POV tries to avoid. When the speaker is

unclear, deep POV uses action tags (i.e., describes what the speaker is doing) instead of dialogue tags.

Normal:

"How could you let it fall apart like this?" Carolyn shouted into her phone.

"I never wanted it. Dad just gave it to me," Gary said from the other end of the line.

The server walked over to Carolyn's table, and Carolyn held up her coffee cup. Instead, the server said, "Ma'am, I'm gonna need you to keep it down."

Carolyn glared at her, then said into the phone, "I have to call you back."

Deep POV:

Carolyn raised her voice. "How could you let it fall apart like this?"

"I never wanted it. Dad just gave it to me."

The server appeared, and Carolyn held up her coffee cup.

"Ma'am, I'm gonna need you to keep it down."

Carolyn glared. "Gary, I have to call you back."

The Effect:

Removing the dialogue tags prevents the narrator from breaking the fourth wall ("hey, reader, this dialogue was said by this guy") and allows the reader to remain in the action of the story without the narrator interjecting.

Keep in Mind:

Action tags can come before or after the dialogue (or not at all), and mixing up the order can help keep the conversation from falling into a singsongy rhythm. Also be careful whenever you mention more than one person in the action tag to ensure that readers will understand who the speaker is. (For example, who's speaking? Landon handed the screwdriver to Howard. "Thanks for your help.") **Context can help with this issue. Also, a good rule of thumb is to place the speaker closest to the dialogue** ("Thanks for your help." Landon handed the screwdriver to Howard). **However, if the speaker clearly dominates the action, then placement of the characters relative to the dialogue probably doesn't matter.** (Landon handed the screwdriver to Howard and let out a deep breath. "Thanks for your help.")

3. **Avoid thought tags.** Like dialogue tags, thought tags interject the narrator's voice and remind the reader who is telling the story.

Normal:

Carolyn paced on the porch, waiting for the contractor, and thought about the consequences she would suffer at her job if she were over an hour late. She dialed his number. *Answer . . . answer . . .,* she thought.

She suddenly stopped pacing when she felt one of the boards start to give beneath her. She looked closely, saw a soft spot, and thought, *That's all I need—to put a foot through one of these boards.*

Deep POV:

Carolyn paced the porch.

"Why are contractors always late? If I were over an hour late to an appointment, I'd lose my job. But not contractors! What's up with that?"

She dialed the phone. Answer . . . answer . . . "No answer. Great."

She stopped pacing when one of the boards started to give way beneath her.

Well, that's all I need, to put a foot through one of these boards.

The Effect:

Again, by keeping the narrator out of it, we're able to allow readers to get into the POV character's head—literally when it comes to thoughts—and to let them stay there without being pulled out to get information from the narrator. It's like the difference between swimming, snorkeling, and scuba diving. Swimming is normal writing with the narrator's interjections as breaths of air. Snorkeling is *show, don't tell*—you can keep your head under for a long time, but eventually you have to look up. In deep POV, readers are taken to the depths of the sea with a continuous supply of oxygen.

4. **No hedging language.** Consider the difference between he seemed distracted and he kept looking at the door. How about she looked nervous and she twisted her wedding ring and checked the clock on the wall? First of all, he seemed distracted and she looked nervous tell—the narrator is spoon-feeding the character's emotional state to the readers. But also remember #3 in the previous section—everything is described from the POV character's perspective. So if the POV character thinks he's distracted or she's nervous, then he's distracted and she's nervous—drop the "seem" and the "look" and tell it like it is. Unless the POV character has doubts about the reality before them, describe situations and characters using straightforward language that indicates the POV character's perception.

Also avoid phrases like *started to* and *began to*—He started to drive away and then he was gone. Just state it outright—He drove away. This makes the action more immediate and engaging. (**NOTE:** He started to drive away, but she stopped him is perfectly fine because he doesn't actually drive away.)

Normal:

Carolyn walked the contractor around and through the house. He seemed to be paying attention, though he rarely spoke, just *mm-hmm*'d a lot. In each room, he pulled out a laser device and started to take measurements while Carolyn described what she wanted. Although it was a pretty one-sided conversation, by the time they were done, they seemed to be on the same page regarding Carolyn's goals for the restoration.

Deep POV:

Carolyn walked the contractor around and through the house.

"So here in the kitchen I'd like to have a nice big island with plenty of storage."

"Mm-hmm."

Mm-hmm? What's with all the mm-hmms? Is he even paying attention? And here comes the laser thingamajig gadget again.

"Does that store all the measurements from all the rooms?"

"Mm-hmm."

Carolyn's whole body clenched. She took a deep breath, held it, then let it out at the count of ten. She tapped her fingers against her thigh and counted the ceiling tiles.

How many measurements does he need?

He stopped measuring and pushed buttons on the device. "Give me a few minutes. I'll be right back."

Aha! Real words!

Carolyn pulled herself up onto the counter and swung her legs while she checked her email.

Delete. Delete. Spam. Promo. Ad. Political BS. Delete. Delete.

The contractor returned and handed Carolyn a notebook. "Here are some rough sketches."

Carolyn flipped through the pages and her mouth dropped open.

Holy crap! These are perfect!

The Effect:

In the "normal" version, the contractor "seemed to be paying attention," he "started to take measurements," and "they seemed to be on the same page." This is all hedging language. For the deep POV version, we can't just let the narrator make these indecisive declarations. So instead, we have Carolyn question whether the contractor is paying attention. We have Carolyn observing the contractor taking measurements (not "starting to" take measurements—actually taking them). And we have the contractor presenting his sketches and Carolyn reacting, showing that they are, indeed, on the same page. Through the rewrite, we leave behind a vague description of what's happening in the house and instead present a scene in which we get all the same information, plus we get to spend some time in Carolyn's head.

5. **Avoid sensory/emotion indicators.** There's a big difference between *telling that* a character experienced or felt something and *describing what* the character experienced or felt. Verbs that indicate the five senses or emotions—he saw, she heard, he felt—tell, and they can interrupt the reader's engagement with the story. In chapter 9, I compared she heard a wolf howl and the hairs on the back of her neck bristled as a wolf howled in the distance. Not surprisingly, chapter 9 is the *show, don't*

tell chapter, because avoiding sensory/emotion indicators is a classic aspect of *show, don't tell*—and it applies even more in deep POV. So instead of using those words, simply describe what's happening—or let the character describe it—so readers can see what the character sees, hear what the character hears, and feel what the character feels.

Normal:

Carolyn stood in the middle of her gutted living room. She smelled the dust that floated through a sunbeam coming from the uncovered window and felt the warmth on her skin. She imagined the room as it had looked when she was a kid, and she remembered playing hide-and-seek. She stepped to where the couch had been and saw a faint outline in the wood floor—the remnants of a cup of juice she'd spilled and tried to hide under a towel when she was seven.

Deep POV:

Carolyn stood in the middle of her living room. "So that's what they mean by 'down to the studs.' Remember when this room had curtains and carpet . . . and drywall? . . . I really have to stop talking to myself."

A sunbeam transected the room, and Carolyn swatted at the dust particles floating through it. "Musty dust. Check. Sun cooking the room through bare windows. Check."

She turned from one side of the room to another. "Let's see . . . the couch was there." She pointed to her left. "Grandma's chair. Grandpa's chair." She pointed to each location.

She stepped to where the couch had been and leaned down toward a spot in the floor. "Uh-oh. Water mark. Wait, is that where I spilled juice when I was, what, seven? Jeez, that stuff really does go right through the carpet. I probably should have told Grandma about it instead of just covering it with a towel. Oops!"

The Effect:

Who doesn't prefer a character talking to themselves to simply being told about what the character is experiencing? The description is OK, but getting a tour of that room by Carolyn herself as she relives some of her memories of it? Priceless (wink, wink). In the "normal" description, Carolyn smells the dust, she feels the warmth, and she sees the stain on the floor. In the deep POV rewrite, she informs readers herself about the dust, the warmth, and the stain, making it unnecessary for the narrator to tell readers about them.

You can tell readers that a character saw something or heard something or felt something, but that's just giving them information. When you show readers what the character saw or heard or felt, you pull those readers into the story and, when using deep POV especially, into the POV character's head, so that readers can experience those sights, sounds, smells, and feelings too.

6. **Use active voice.** Active voice is immediate and has movement to it, while passive voice is delayed and slow. In deep POV, you want to always be moving forward. Also, for any action that directly involves the POV character, active voice keeps that character front and center, which keeps readers focused on them and how they're experiencing the story.

Passive Narration:

Carolyn stopped at the end of the driveway as the last of the landscaping trucks left. The new sod was laid; the gravel driveway, which wrapped around to the back of the house, was now finished; and her grandparents' house was finally restored. Carolyn was thrilled, and she couldn't wait to schedule the movers.

Active Deep POV Narration:

Carolyn stopped at the end of the driveway. She waved as the last of the landscapers drove away. Fresh sod now wrapped around the house, and the gravel driveway cut through it and wound around to the back.

"Grandma and Grandpa, this is for you."

She grinned and dialed her phone.

"O'Ryan Storage and Moving. How can I help you?"

"Hi, I need to schedule moving services."

In deep POV, the narrator is not just an unknown entity. The narrator has no voice at all because the story is told in the POV character's voice and from that character's perspective. The POV character colors everything with their thoughts, opinions, beliefs, ideas, emotions, experiences, and so on. Simple descriptions become interpretations, and the story unfolds for the readers just as it does for the POV character.

Just like *show, don't tell*, deep POV requires a lot of practice to do it well. You might find that it's easier to go in and out of deep POV, using it only in scenes where it makes the most sense and has the most impact. And if you're new to deep POV, you might try practicing it on short fiction (flash fiction / short stories) before you try to tackle a full-length novel (baby steps!). Finally, consider trying to find a writing buddy who understands deep POV and can evaluate your attempts as you go. This will help you see what you're doing well and where you need more practice, thus improving your deep POV skills.

If deep POV intrigues you, give it a try and see how you do. You might find you really enjoy it. Just don't expect it to be easy and don't expect to be great at it right away. But hey, deep POV is still not terribly commonplace in mainstream fiction, so it could become your signature as an author. Who knows?!

Practice Deep POV

Rewrite the following scene using deep POV. Be imaginative and add whatever details you want. See my rewrite on page 237.

Dionne lit a candle and walked into the kitchen. She surveyed what little she could in the darkness of the sudden power outage. She hated summer storm season and shuddered at the sound of the howling wind outside. She could hear the clanking of the chains from the swing set in the backyard as the swings crashed into each other. Dionne considered the joy she would experience trying to untangle them tomorrow, and she made a mental note to sell it now that the kids had gotten too old for it.

Her phone buzzed and she put it on speaker.

"Hello, Mom," she said softly.

"I heard there are power outages there. Do you have power?" her mom said unnecessarily loudly. She never could get it through her head that you don't have to yell into a cell phone.

"No, but I'm fine. I have plenty of candles to get me through the night," she said, trying not to sound too weary.

"Are you sure? Is Carter there to help you?"

"No, the kids are with their dad this weekend." She decided she was glad for that. No reason for them to go through this hassle.

"Well, you call them if you need them," her mom commanded.

"I will, Mom. I better go. I don't want to run down my phone battery."

She got off the call and thought about how much she loved her mom—and how glad she was her mom lived three states away!

Chapter 12

Avoiding Clichés

A cliché is something that has been overused to the point of losing its impact and, in some cases, its original meaning. Clichés can be words, phrases, plot conventions, character traits, and even settings. Anything that is used to the point of utter predictability is a cliché. But more important than predictability is the issue of originality, and that's where clichés cause the most problems.

Clichés are tricky because we use them all the time in speech and in writing. They are fallbacks that we cling to with the assumption that other people will automatically understand what we mean without further description or explanation. If I say, "He fell for the scam hook, line, and sinker," chances are you know what I mean—that he accepted what he was told without questioning any of it. You may not have any idea where the phrase came from or what "hook, line, and sinker" refers to, but you still get the gist.

That's how clichés come to be. They are recognizable words, phrases, characteristics, themes, and the like that carry a particular meaning, connotation, or symbolism that most everyone understands. Thus they get repeated *a lot*. So much so, in fact, that eventually they lose their initial impact and become tired.

Types of Clichés

We're going to cover two basic types of clichés: linguistic clichés (words/phrases) and literary clichés (plots/characters/themes). We'll be focusing on linguistic clichés, but let's take a moment to discuss literary clichés first.

Literary Clichés

We use literary clichés when we fall back on overused plots, characters, settings, and themes without trying to make them unique in any way. These clichés make the story predictable because we've seen them so many times.

Consider the Cinderella story, the rags-to-riches story, or the mistaken identity romance story. Consider themes like *love conquers all* or *believe in yourself*. Consider the downtrodden underdog, the shy late bloomer, or the damsel in distress (yuck). Consider thunderstorms in, well, anything—thunderstorms are terribly overused.

These are all literary clichés. We've seen them a million times in books, in movies, and on TV, and the only way to use them effectively is to turn them inside out and remove predictability.

For example, rain is often used as a downer to reflect a bad circumstance or a sad character. *Gene Kelly danced in it.* That's how you take something tired and turn it into something fresh and rewarding. Maybe your downtrodden underdog actually loses (but learns and grows anyway, obviously). Maybe your Cinderella spurns the handsome prince and opens her own bakery. Maybe your damsel frees herself from the train tracks and kicks a little a—. Well, you get what I'm saying.

Clichés can appear in your plot, your characters, your environment/setting, and your themes. Make them your own, however, and your readers will enjoy the unpredictability of your stories.

Clichés Versus Tropes

I don't want to offend anyone, but here's the bottom line: Tropes are literary clichés. That's not an insult, just a fact. Tropes are also very important if you're writing to market.

Wait a second, you're thinking, *you just said literary clichés are bad.* Yes, I did. And yes, they are—*if you don't do something interesting with them.* Fans of specific genres tend to really want to see specific tropes. So if you're writing to market, you have to include the tropes that your target readers want. That's OK. Just be original about it (and don't call them clichés—call them tropes).

For example, what would a Western novel be without cattle rustlers and gunfighters? These are very tired, overused Western characters, but fans of Westerns can't get enough of them. If you want to write a Western that reaches the largest possible reader base, you'd best have these types of characters in your book. But they don't have to be just like every other cattle rustler or gunfighter ever written, especially if they're among your main characters. Find a way to make them unique so that cattle rustling or gunfighting becomes the least interesting thing about them.

The most important lesson to be learned here is that, whether you call them literary clichés or tropes, you need to make them your own.

Linguistic Clichés

These are the clichés of words and phrases. In my research, I've found it rare for anyone to refer to them as "linguistic clichés." I'm not saying I made up the term, but most folks just call them clichés. I'm using the term *linguistic cliché* simply to distinguish them from literary clichés.

Not! Here we have an example of the rare single-word cliché, just in case you couldn't think of one. Most linguistic clichés are phrases, and there are hundreds of them, maybe even thousands. If you go to be-a-better-writer.com, you can find a list of 681 of them.[1] Actually, there are a few repeats, so it's really more like 677. Still, that's a heck of a list, and it isn't even comprehensive.

Any phrase or word can become a cliché simply through overuse. Every time a word or phrase becomes so popular that it seems like everyone is saying it, that word or phrase has become a cliché. *Right?!* (Oh, look, another single-word cliché. Yay, me!) Linguistic clichés are usually metaphors or idioms that have a specific meaning beyond the meaning of the words themselves. Raining cats and dogs is a good example. This phrase is a metaphor that does not mean that dogs and cats are literally falling from the sky. It means that a heavy rain is falling. You knew that, of course, because it's a cliché and you've heard it eight million times.

The Problem with Clichés

Aside from the fact that we hear them so often, clichés have a multitude of issues. I'll be focusing on linguistic clichés, but these problems can apply to literary clichés as well.

Clichés Are Boring

Because we hear them all the time, clichés are pretty blah, just there taking up space. If I say, "It rained cats and dogs for hours," does that interest you? What if I say, "A waterfall cascaded down the window as rain continued to hammer the roof"? Huh? Better, right? Avoiding the cliché and giving a detailed description really wakes up the narrative and makes it much more interesting to read.

Clichés Are Unoriginal

One of the worst offenses of clichés is that they are someone else's words. You probably don't have the slightest idea who originally said any of them (a lot of them were Shakespeare, by the way), but still, you didn't make them up. They aren't your words, so why would you want them in your story? Be original. Maybe you'll turn a phrase that becomes a cliché someday.

Clichés Are Vague

Sure, you know what *raining cats and dogs* means, but you don't get a full picture of what's happening. Heavy rain. That's all this phrase tells you. Is it storming or just raining? Is the wind blowing? What types of cats and dogs are we talking about here? I want more information. I'm sure you do too. So skip the cliché and give a description that is actually *descriptive*.

Clichés Make Assumptions

Earlier, I used the cliché *hook, line, and sinker* as an example. Do you know what it means? I assumed that you do, but maybe you don't. It's tough for me to make my point if I'm using a tired phrase that you've never heard before or just never really understood. "Hook, line, and sinker" is a fishing reference—a fish that breaks the line and gets free swims off with the hook, the line, and the sinker, which has come to mean "everything, no exceptions." Maybe you knew the fishing reference. Maybe you didn't but you understood the cliché anyway. Or maybe the whole thing was foreign to you. That's one of the problems with using clichés. As writers, we cannot predict what our readers will or will not understand.

Clichés Are Lazy

Again, if you're falling back on someone else's words, you aren't doing your job as a writer. It's time to dig in and find your creative mojo. Do the work and make it great. You have it in you—you know you do. Otherwise, you wouldn't be trying to write a book or a short story or a poem or whatever it is you're trying to write. Writing is hard. Most anyone who's ever tried it will tell you that. But the work is worth it when you can look at your final product and know that it's 100 percent you. Give yourself that gift. (The same thing applies to AI-generated content. Lazy, lazy, lazy! There, I said it!)

Clichés Tell

Here we are again. Telling. Take the examples from the "Clichés Are Boring" section again. "It rained cats and dogs for hours" is telling. "A waterfall cascaded down the window as rain continued to hammer the roof" is showing. Yes, please!

Clichés Are Disappointing

Finally, using clichés may disappoint your readers. They've picked up your story in the hopes of getting a new and interesting experience. Even readers who want tropes, tropes, tropes want those tropes in a unique way with original writing. You're asking readers to trust that you will make them laugh, cry, gasp, scream, swoon, and so on to their utter delight. Keep your promise and nix the clichés.

Avoiding Clichés

Here are a few strategies for getting away from linguistic clichés:

Show. Don't Tell.

Need I say more?

Consider What the Cliché Means

Ask yourself what it is you're trying to say. Describe it to yourself, then consider if any of the words you used to describe the cliché can be used *instead of* the cliché. For example, as we already discussed, *raining cats and dogs* could mean rain, heavy rain, downpour, monsoon, rainstorm, deluge … Any of these words strike you as a better choice than *raining cats and dogs*? (The correct answer is yes!)

Decide If the Cliché Is Necessary

Another thing to consider is whether you even need to say what you're trying to say. Maybe we don't really need to know that it's raining outside. If you're struggling to get rid of a cliché, ask yourself whether you need it at all. Maybe the best solution is to just delete it and move on.

Consult the Thesaurus

Despite what Stephen King has said (what does he know?), the thesaurus can be your best friend when you're trying to replace a cliché. On thesaurus.com and similar sites, you can plug in your cliché and find alternatives.

Create Your Own Cliché

Instead of saying, "He avoided asparagus like the plague," say something like "He avoided asparagus like he avoided his uncle during the Super Bowl—*entirely*." Your made-up cliché, like this example, may require more context than the original cliché would, but that's OK. The point is to take those pesky old clichés and turn them into something original. Instead of being stuck in the tired and worn-out, you'll get points for creativity. Bring on the five-star reviews!

When to Use Clichés

Now, I imagine you're thinking something like "Um, Julie, you've used tons of clichés in this book. What gives?" Well, of course I have. Everyone uses them. That's how they become clichés.

Like every other piece of writing advice ever given, you must take this one with the proverbial grain of salt. Yes, it's best to avoid clichés for the variety of reasons given here, but that doesn't mean you can't ever use them. There will be times when the perfect cliché is the perfect match for what you need, and that's just fine and dandy. The more you avoid them, the more effective they will be when you don't. Just be sure to use them only when they are the perfect fit and not because you simply couldn't think of—or didn't want to take the time to think of—something original.

Practice Replacing Clichés

Rewrite the following sentences and remove or replace the clichés. See my answers on page 238.

1. The cops on my favorite show are always *armed to the teeth*.

2. Look at that baby! She's *cute as a button*!

3. There's no talking to him right now. He's *high as a kite*.

4. They were determined to *make the best of a bad situation*.

5. Let me take *a shot in the dark* and say . . . you *woke up on the wrong side of the bed* this morning.

6. My grandparents have always been like *two peas in a pod*.

7. It doesn't matter which option you choose. It's *six of one, half dozen of the other.*

8. C'mon! Don't be so sensitive. I'm just *yanking your chain!*

9. Look at all this corrosion. These batteries are *older than dirt.*

10. Fighting this merger will definitely be an *uphill battle.*

Chapter 13

Hire an Editor

Many authors don't realize the value of editing, especially if they are hoping to publish traditionally (with a traditional book publisher versus hybrid or self-publishing). And many authors who do understand the value don't know how to find quality editors or exactly what type of editing they need. If you're among either of these groups, I hope this chapter helps.

I can spot a self-published book from a mile away. OK, that's hyperbole. Not all self-published books are so easily recognized as such, but many—and I mean *many*—are obvious. And it's not that no publishing house has ever put out a bad book, but they are far less likely to publish the plot holes, inconsistencies, poor grammar, bad formatting, and overall amateurness of a *stereotypical* self-published book. To stand out from the crowd in the self-publishing world means to blend in with the traditionally published crowd, and that means editors, editors, editors!

But even traditional publishers are beginning to demand a greater amount of editing from authors. Some publishers won't even consider a book that hasn't been independently edited at least once. Hiring an editor puts your best foot forward and shows publishers that you're committed to your book. (It also removes some of their financial burden, which is quite the bonus for them.)

Self-Editing Is Not Enough

Now, you may be thinking that you have all the necessary skills to edit your own book. Maybe you're even a professional editor. Good for you! Still, don't take this personally, but *you are your own worst enemy* when it comes to evaluating the quality of your own writing. No matter how well prepared you are. No matter how well you know your subject, your characters, your settings, your plot. No matter how good you are with grammar. *No matter what.* You are simply too close to it to be able to evaluate it. You cannot look at it with the eyes of a reader, and you cannot see the problems, not entirely. You know it too well, and you know what you mean.

Consider the following sentence.

Jordan made a sandwich for Lily before she told Max about the recital.

Look at the sentence and ask yourself these questions: Who is Max? Who talked to him? Who had the recital?

Now, I wrote this sentence, so I know exactly what it means, and I can tell you that if you think Jordan talked to her husband, Max, about their daughter's recital, you're wrong. But as the author, I may not realize that there's ambiguity here. It makes sense to me!

An editor might suggest that I rewrite the sentence as follows:

Jordan made a sandwich for her little sister, Lily, who couldn't wait to brag to their neighbor, Max, about Jordan's amazing recital.

We now know the correct answers to those questions because the copy is no longer vague.

My experiences while first writing this book are the perfect example of what I'm trying to explain. I wrote each chapter until I thought it was complete and understandable. Then I showed the chapters one by one to my critiquing writing group. I was repeatedly surprised by sections I thought might be confusing that everyone understood just fine and sections I thought were solid that actually confused everyone. And, yes, I did work with a professional copy editor on both editions of the book, and I'm grateful for every comment they made (not to mention my proofreader!). This book is far better than it would have been if I had only edited it myself.

That's not to say that there isn't a lot you can do to avoid issues, and the more you learn about writing, the better at it you will be. And the better you are at writing, the less your editor will have to do for you. But you still need an editor. And a proofreader. For the love of Pete, if you're self-publishing, don't forget the proofreader.

What Editors Do

There are different types of editors, and their responsibilities vary depending on what type of editing they do. However, all editors exist to help improve an author's writing. An editor may check some or all of the following on a job: readability, consistency, grammar and style, plot development, character development, genre-specific requirements, voice, point of view, tense, and on and on.

Generally speaking, all editors read your manuscript at least twice and make suggestions for changes based on their expertise. The exact deliverables vary, but in most cases, your manuscript (or book layout if it's proofreading) will be returned with comments and inline suggestions, which you will review, accept or reject as you see fit, and use to help you make needed revisions.

Types of Editing

I've done a lot of research on this subject, and I've often found it confusing. For some reason, not everyone seems to agree on all the definitions and terms, and what I'm about to describe might not jibe with how others define them.

For the sake of simplicity, let's just agree that I'm right and they're wrong. (Oh, come on. It's my book!) The fact is, there is no industry standard for the various types and levels of editing, so discuss your needs with your chosen editor and let them help you decide what service(s) they should provide.

Please note that you may require more than one type of editing, and particularly if you're new to writing, you might even require all of them. Needs vary per author and per project. Consider where you are in the process, what you're struggling with (if anything), how confident you are in the quality of your writing, and how much change you're willing to make. Hire accordingly.

Developmental Editing

I like to use a forest metaphor to explain the different levels of editing, and by this metaphor, developmental editing is the level that deals with the forest itself. What does that mean? It means that developmental editing deals with the big-picture issues of a story—the plot, characters, story arc, theme, and so on. These editors are not concerned with the minutiae of grammar, punctuation, and spelling, and they're only somewhat concerned with your line-by-line writing. When you hire a developmental editor, you're hiring someone to help you flesh out your story and ensure that it's easy to follow, that the characters are fully formed, that the story makes sense, and that the whole thing is poised to achieve your goals. A developmental editor works with the author late in the writing stage or, more likely, after completion of the full draft, usually after the author has done a round or two of revisions on their own.

Let's say you have the book written, but something's missing. You can't put your finger on it. You've gotten yourself from point A to point B, but you had to jump over some mighty big holes to get there. You know something (or many somethings) is off, but you don't know what it is. Frustration is bringing you down and you're about to scrap the whole thing.

You could hire beta readers, and that's a good idea, but it may not be enough. Beta readers don't do what developmental editors do, not entirely. Beta readers give their reactions as readers, but developmental editors can give you feedback that goes beyond reader reactions to industry expectations and norms. Plus, developmental editors don't just give inline comments within your manuscript.

They deliver (or at least they *should* deliver) a detailed editorial letter that discusses the pros and cons of your current draft, gives well-thought-out suggestions for improvements, and—if the editor is top-notch—helps you learn and improve as a writer overall, not just for the current manuscript.

As I mentioned, developmental editors do not evaluate grammar or drill down into the line-by-line details of how the story is written. These editors concentrate on plot, characters, themes, tropes, and the like. Is the story whole? Are the characters fully formed? Is the plot confusing or hard to follow? Have you satisfied the expectations of readers in your genre? These broad-spectrum questions, and others, are answered by developmental editors in an attempt to ensure that your forest (remember the metaphor?) is full and lush and beautiful.

When you hire a developmental editor, make sure they're an expert in your category (fiction/memoir/nonfiction) and genre. Because they're essentially helping you write the book, they need to understand how your type of book should be written.

For example, let's say you're writing a sci-fi novel, and you want to appeal to the mass sci-fi market. An editor who specializes in sci-fi can evaluate whether you've effectively used a variety of sci-fi tropes, if the "sci" in your sci-fi is sound, if your story is believable, if your characters fit the genre, and even if your story is the appropriate length for this market. The right editor can help you avoid errors that might turn off avid sci-fi readers and can give you a fighting chance at being noticed within that market.

Developmental Editing Versus Coaching

Coaching usually takes place while you're writing the first draft. Say you have a great idea, but you don't know where to start. Or maybe you've started, but now you're hopelessly stalled. A writing coach can help you figure out what you're missing so you can keep writing. Coaching and developmental editing have some overlap, and some editors offer both services—coaching for finishing the draft and developmental editing for filling in the gaps. If you're new to writing and really struggling to find your voice, consider hiring a writing coach.

Line Editing / Substantive Editing / Content Editing

These terms are often used interchangeably, though some editors define each term very differently. Again, there are no industry standards, but most editors would agree that I'm about to describe line editing, even if they don't agree that substantive or content editing are the same thing. And even if they do lump these terms together, they probably use the term "line editing" instead of one of the others.

Line editing is a deeper dive into the text than developmental editing. In other words, it's less concerned with the story itself and more concerned about how you've put words together in order to tell the story. Think of it this way: If developmental editing is all about the forest as a whole, then line editing is all about the trees.

In line editing, the editor looks at the copy line by line (hence the name) and evaluates if the writing is clear, concise, and complete. This editor looks for inconsistencies, missing information, confusing organization (e.g., "Move this description to before the dialogue because Jonas refers to it during the conversation"), and general issues with the writing itself. Line editors don't look at the ideas and the plan so much as they look at how the story is executed. These are the editors who are most likely to check for excessive use of adverbs, showing versus telling, effective dialogue, verbosity, clarity, clichés, offensive or biased language, mixed metaphors, repetition, choppiness, awkward phrasing, and so on. They help improve the flow and readability of the writing.

Line editors work on the draft after developmental editing or once the story itself is solid. Line editing earlier than this would be a waste of time and money because if the story isn't nailed down yet, big revisions will likely be made that would wipe out a lot of the line editor's work. So this review happens on a later draft, but not the final draft.

Line editors may look for errors and inconsistencies in grammar and style, but that's not really their focus. They're more interested in how the story is told—the quality of the overall writing as opposed to comma usage. For that, you want a copy editor.

Copyediting / Mechanical Editing

Copy editors don't analyze the story itself (well, sure they do, but that's not their focus). They're more concerned with word usage, grammar, style, spelling, formatting, consistency, and, to a lesser extent, overall readability. Small rewrites—to, say, get rid of those last pesky adverbs—are not uncommon through copyediting; however, large rewrites are almost unheard of at this stage (unless something is egregiously wrong with your story).

If developmental editors are concerned with the forest and line editors focus on the trees, then copy editors worry about the leaves—the small details that make a forest full and gorgeous and a story readable, understandable, and professional.

Copyediting, as a general rule, takes place on a draft that is almost ready to publish but needs to be polished.

Proofreading

Technically, proofreading is not a type of editing because *proofreaders don't edit*. All they do is look for errors. And while they may evaluate the copy beyond that, they don't point out issues unless they're really, really bad, because . . .

Proofreading is the very last review before publishing. If you're self-publishing, get your book formatted and ready to go, then, before you upload your files for publishing, have a proofreader check them. (Traditional publishers do this for you, by the way.)

Proofreaders look for misspellings, grammar and style errors, typos, and inconsistencies. They check formatting, footnotes/endnotes, captions, headings, page numbers (in tables of contents, indexes, etc.), running heads, margins, and so on. If your editor created a style sheet, your proofreader will ensure that everything on it is being followed consistently as well.

Copy editors check for these things too, but they do it before the manuscript is formatted for publishing, and mistakes can be made during the revision and formatting processes. That's what proofreaders look for. Also, copy editors assess the readability of the text. Proofreaders don't. So while these two evaluations may seem to be the same, they have very necessary and important differences.

Proofreaders ensure that your self-published book doesn't *look* self-published (by catching errors and inconsistencies in the formatting) or *read* as self-published (by catching lingering typos and other errors). And if you've ever read a self-published book that wasn't professionally proofread, you know exactly what I mean.

Professional Versus Amateur

Is your Aunt Jeanine really good at grammar? Maybe she's a retired

English teacher and an avid reader. She has time to kill and she loves you. Sure, she'll proofread your book for you (for free!). Sounds like a great deal, doesn't it?

Aunt Jeanine might do a pretty good job too, but if she isn't a professional editor or proofreader, then you're selling yourself short. Not only do professionals have abundant experience in the field, but they have an industry-specific knowledge base and a community of professionals backing up their every move.

As mentioned, professional developmental editors often specialize in certain genres and can help you ensure that your story meets the expectations of your reader base (if you're writing to market). And even if you aren't writing to market, an editor who specializes in your genre will be more adept at spotting problems or inconsistencies. Professional line editors and copy editors master the rules in particular style guides, like *Chicago* for fiction and general nonfiction or industry-specific guides (like AMA's or APA's) for more technical writing. Professional proofreaders also bring a unique ability to the mix. They are extremely good with detail and can catch the smallest problems—like a double space between words—that Aunt Jeanine is simply not trained for.

If you want to roll the dice with nonprofessionals, you certainly have that option. Just be aware that you may not be getting the best guidance and your book could suffer for it. To get the most out of your writing and your editing experience, hire professionals.

Editing Costs

Costs will vary depending on the service or services provided and the length of your story. Developmental editing is the most expensive and the price goes down as the service gets more detailed.

Proofreading is generally least expensive. I don't know why this is. It almost seems backward, but that's the way it usually works.

I can't tell you how much it will cost, because that will depend entirely on the editor you hire. I can tell you that higher costs don't necessarily ensure better service; however, the more experience an editor has, the more they are likely to charge. Newer editors will tend to be less expensive. A great resource for pricing norms is the Editorial Freelancers Association (the-efa.org), which publishes average rates, based on member surveys, for a variety of editorial services. Keep in mind, though, that these prices are just averages based on a small percentage of the editorial community, not industry standards, and they're rates for *freelancers*. An editing company is likely to have higher prices because of higher overhead.

I recommend that you find an editor who charges based on word count or page count (which is ultimately a word count—one page usually equals 250–300 words). Hourly rates are tricky, because each editor is different. We read, evaluate, and mark up manuscripts at different speeds, but who's to say that one speed is better than another? A faster editor will cost less, but does that mean the service is better or worse than a slower editor? There's simply no way to evaluate that. Per-word rates make this question obsolete.

Please note that many editors will charge a per-word rate for their editing time but will charge an additional per-hour rate for meetings to discuss the work. This is normal and should not be cause for alarm. However, be careful to stay on task in these meetings and end them at the agreed-upon time. If a meeting runs over, you will likely be charged extra for the additional time. There is nothing underhanded about this practice. You just need to be aware of it and take caution to keep meetings to their scheduled length.

Beware rates that seem too good to be true. If you find an editor willing to line edit an 80,000-word novel for $500, run away. Chances are this person is either very inexperienced or not a native English speaker (i.e., they are from a foreign country). Be cognizant of who you're hiring and expect to pay a decent wage for their hard work.

Where to Find Editors

Freelance editors can be found through a Google search or on social media. Most professionals have a profile on Facebook, Instagram, or LinkedIn. You can also check out editing groups like the Editorial Freelancers Association (the-efa.org) and ACES: The Society for Editing (aceseditors.org). These groups are specific to US editors. Other groups include the Chartered Institute of Editing and Proofreading in the UK (ciep.uk) and Editors Canada (editors.ca).

If you want an editor who specializes in a particular genre, be sure to include that genre name in your search (e.g., "romance editors"). If you're looking for a proofreader, search specifically by that name. While you may find proofreaders via an "editor" search, you'll find more through a "proofreaders" search.

Freelance Worksites

I'm referring to sites like Fiverr and Upwork. These sites feature quite a few providers from outside the US. If you're comfortable with that, then fine. However, I do encourage you to consider the impact on your writing if you hire a provider who is not a native English speaker. I'm not saying that these editors are incapable, but I think you will have a harder time finding the high quality of service your words deserve. And even the native English speakers are more likely to be fluent in British (or closer to British) English if they aren't from the US. There are significant differences between US and UK English in grammar and style rules and how words are used. My recommendation is that you find a native US editor. You will probably pay more, but you'll get a more appropriate language experience.

Additionally, these sites are more likely to feature part-time providers who are just looking to make some extra money. There's certainly nothing wrong with that, and I have no doubt that many of those folks are very good at what they offer. However, I do encourage you to seek out a provider who does this work *for a living*. First of all, you will be helping someone work for themselves and be independent. Second, you will be hiring someone who lives and breathes the editing life. Why wouldn't you want that person in your corner?

One last note here: If you do decide to look for an editor on one of these sites, please pay very close attention to the providers' reviews and experience. Don't just hire based on price. This, of course, is good advice whether you're on a worksite or not, but it's particularly important here because anyone can hang a shingle on these sites, regardless of experience or ability. Many very skilled, talented, and reliable providers find work through these sites, but you have to do your due diligence and ensure that you're finding *those* people.

A Note About Editing Software / AI

Editing software is great and can be useful, but it is not a replacement for a live person who understands nuance and inflection and can choose when exceptions to the rules should be made. Services like Grammarly and AutoCrit can be used as part of the self-editing phase before submitting to an editor. They should not be used *in place of* the editor. I've encountered far too many examples of AI misreading or misunderstanding my writing and making suggestions for changes that would either make the text grammatically incorrect (hello?!) or cause the text to not make sense or to mean something other than what I intended. So beware leaning on these services too heavily. AI is great. *People are better.*

And while I'm nagging you about AI, let me quickly caution you against using AI to help you write your book (research, yes; editing, yes; writing—no!). First of all, AI plagiarizes—like mad! And even if, at some point, AI stops doing that and starts writing content out of the blue, it's still not your words. And publishers and booksellers, like Amazon, are now scanning books in search of AI-generated content. If you use it, and especially if you use a lot of it (which everyone defines differently), you could suffer serious consequences, not the least of which could include being banned from selling on Amazon and other sites. So please write your own book. The alternative is too risky and too dishonest.

Hiring an Editor: Information to Provide and Questions to Ask

When you find an editor you want to reach out to, you need to have some basic information about your project ready to go.

Potential Editors Need to Know

- Type of writing: Fiction, narrative nonfiction, prescriptive non-fiction, technical, and so on
- Genre: Romance, sci-fi, mystery, memoir, and so on
- Word count: If you're still writing, you can give a ballpark figure.
- Service needed or type of editing required: If you aren't sure,

that's OK; see the "Questions to Ask Potential Editors" section.

+ Approximate timeline: When will the draft be ready to review (if it isn't already) and when do you want to have the editing completed (if you're on a specific timeline)?

Questions to Ask Potential Editors

NOTE: Check their websites or worksite / social media profiles for answers first. Ask only those questions that the providers haven't already answered online.

+ What services do you provide?
+ Do you charge a per-word rate or an hourly rate?
+ What are your rates for each service offered? Do you charge extra for meetings?
+ Do you offer discounts for combined services (for example, copyediting plus proofreading)?
+ What is your standard turnaround time for each service?
+ Do you work in the [romance/sci-fi/mystery/memoir/etc.] genre? If so, how much experience do you have in this genre?
+ Do you require a down payment? Is it refundable?
+ Do you require a signed contract?
+ What style (*Chicago* style, Strunk and White, AP, etc.) do you follow?
+ What file type(s) (Word, Google Docs, PDF, etc.) do you work with? (Or, *I use [software name]. Can you work with that?*) (Heads up: They're most likely going to want a Word file.)
+ What is your preferred communication method?
+ Will you do a sample edit of my work? (Note that not all editors will do this. You're basically asking them to do work for free, and many highly experienced editors simply won't do that. This is not a red flag, just a professional choice. If an editor won't do a sample

edit of your work, ask if they have prepared samples or samples of previous work they can share.)

If you aren't sure what service or services you need, describe your project and any issues you've encountered, then ask what service(s) they recommend.

Finally, ask for references. You may or may not decide to contact them, but if you're having trouble choosing a provider, these references might help you make the final decision.

Final Note

You should feel good about the person (or people) you hire. If you don't feel like the editor or proofreader you're talking to is a good fit, then find someone else. Find someone you like or, at the very least, who seems like someone you could like. If something feels off, listen to your gut and keep looking. This is someone you might want to work with for years to come on multiple projects, so don't settle. Find the right fit.

If you hire someone and then decide it's not a good fit, you can always walk away. (You'll still have to pay for services rendered and will likely lose any deposit paid.) You don't have to stick with an editor you don't like. (However, please note that "they don't tell me what I want to hear" is not a good reason not to like them!)

Final Note #2 (I know)

Your editor or proofreader is there to do a job for you, and that person's goal is to use their experience and knowledge to improve your writing. Show them the respect they deserve in this role. If you disagree with them, discuss why they suggested the change and try to understand. If you still disagree, then you can choose not to make the change. If a particular comment upsets you, walk away and come back later with a clearer, calmer head. Try not to make any decisions or send any communications while you're upset.

Belligerence will get you nowhere, and treating your provider disrespectfully may cause them to release you as a client. Mutual respect is the key to a successful working relationship.

Final **Final Note**

Pay your editor in full and on time. This is how they make their living. They've worked hard for you, so do the right thing.

Letter to Readers

If you've read this book, I have to assume that you're a writer, so first let me say how honored I am to be in the company of your creative greatness. Authoring is hard work, and your commitment to learning and growing as a writer by reading resources like this one is to be commended. Congratulations for taking such a valuable step in your writing journey—regardless of where you are on it!

And thank you for letting me come along for the ride, if only briefly. I hope you learned something new—lots of somethings!—and that you found the read easy and *enjoyable*. I strive to teach others in the way that I prefer to learn, with humor and a laid-back vibe. So I hope the book satisfied these requirements for you.

If it did, and if you found the book to be a valuable resource for you as an author, then I humbly ask that you hop onto the site you bought it from, or Goodreads if you didn't buy it online, and leave an honest review. I can't tell you how valuable your input is and how much I appreciate your time!

Cheers!
Julie

Appendix A

Exercise Answers and Examples

For the exercises in which I asked you to rewrite sentences, I've given examples of how this might be done. These examples are merely suggestions. Your rewrites may be quite different from (and better than!) mine. As long as you followed the directions, there are no wrong answers.

To BE or Not to BE?

1. Clair *was* tired so she turned in early.

    Exhausted, Clair decided to turn in early.

    Exhausted, Clair crashed into bed two hours earlier than usual.

    Possible advantages of the second version are the more interesting word choices and the specificity.

2. The banners *were* hung around the town square for the celebration.

    The committee hung banners around the town square for the celebration.

    Ancillary benefit: a change from passive to active voice!

3. *Are* you going to the show with Jessica?

    Did you decide to go to the show with Jessica?

    In most situations, this type of question probably doesn't require any change, but it's good practice anyway.

4. There *are* too many books to fit on this shelf.

    This shelf cannot hold all these books.

    Any time you can remove "there + BE verb," go for it!

5. Lin *is* always trying to outdo his brother.

    Lin always tries to outdo his brother.

    Remember to ask yourself if a present participle (-ing ending) is really necessary and appropriate or if simple past/present/future tense wouldn't be better.

6. I'*m* not a fan of horror movies.
    I don't care for horror movies.
    If the original sentence fits the character's voice well, then there wouldn't be any reason to change a sentence like this one.

7. How did you know she *was* lying?
    How did you know she lied?
    In context, the original wording here might be totally appropriate, so again, check those -ing verbs and determine what's best.

8. Carmine *is* the biggest goofball I've ever met.
    Carmine goofs around better than anyone else I know!

9. The wind *is* really howling tonight.
    Guess what? This sentence doesn't require a change at all. Why? Because "howling" is a current, ongoing action, which means that "is howling" is appropriate in this context.

10. That *was* the best meal I've ever eaten.
    That meal blew my mind, the best I've ever had!

Practice Replacing Descriptors

1. I expected the used car salesman to be *slimy* and *creepy* and a *big fat* liar, but he was *actually really* great.

    I expected a stereotype—a liar who made my skin crawl— but the used car salesman surprised me with his honesty.

    Are you curious why I didn't call out "used car" as a descriptor? Well, "used car" is a compound noun-adjective, and if you recall, I explained that you do not need to replace noun-adjectives because they're usually essential for meaning, as is this one.

2. The *rolling* hills stretched out with their *tall waving* grasses in the *warm* sunshine.

    The sun warmed the grasses that reached toward the heavens and waved at the sky in rhythm with the breeze that rolled across the hills.

3. His new car gleamed *brightly* in *strikingly crisp metallic* black.

    His new car gleamed as the sunlight glinted off the metallic black paint.

    Why didn't I replace "metallic"? Why did I turn "black" from a noun into an adjective? Well, there's a big difference between metallic paint and flat paint, and there's no better way to describe it. "Metallic black" is a description that most readers will understand, and it's simply not necessary to change it. But those adverbs had to go!

4. She bought a variety of *silly* toys and *goofy* prizes for the party.

    She bought a variety of finger puppets, rubber ducks, bubbles, and jump ropes plus candy, stuffed animals, and other prizes for the party.

Being specific is often better than simple description. With this revised sentence, it's not necessary to point out that the toys are silly and the prizes goofy. It's pretty obvious (assuming this is a party for adults).

5. The drive was *boring* and I *nearly* feel asleep at the wheel.
    The drive bored me and I struggled to keep my eyes open.
    Note how I turned my adjective boring *into my verb* bored. *You might be surprised how often a switch like that can be done. I did the same thing in #2.*

6. I'd rather eat *crisp, juicy* cucumber slices than put them on my *puffy* eyes.
    I'd rather crunch into those cucumber slices than de-puff my eyes with them.

7. "Wanna get a drink?" she said as she smiled *openly* and *accidentally* revealed an *unknown* hunk of spinach stuck between her *otherwise perfect* teeth.
    "Wanna get a drink?" she said with a smile that revealed her mouthful of perfect teeth and a hunk of spinach that had lodged itself there.
    I chose to keep the adjective perfect *because it's a common description that would be unnecessarily complex to change.*

8. The *giant brown-and-white* dog lay on the *sun-kissed* patio and napped *peacefully.*
    As the sun kissed the patio, the St. Bernard napped through the afternoon.
    When talking about animals, it often works better to just name the breed or type of animal. For example, don't say "the shiny black cat" when you can just say "the panther." Also, be wary of throwing

in a bunch of descriptors as a way of giving a physical description. It can be tedious, and there's almost always a better way.

9.   He set the *beautiful and ornate* table using his grandparents' *vintage* china.

His grandparents' china, which they'd brought with them from Italy, elevated the beauty of the table setting.

Replacing vintage *with a description of the china's origin not only removes the need for the adjective but also opens up a chance to give more info about these characters—they emigrated from Italy.*

10. "Grab that *big* book off the *top* shelf. No, the *red* one. The *big red* one!"

Remember when I said that most of the time the rules go out the window for dialogue? I meant it. People speak the way they speak. No changes are needed here.

Changing Passive to Active

Notice how often the answer to passive voice is to just swap around the sentence so that the object takes its rightful place as the subject.

1. Why *were* Christians *thrown* to the lions in ancient Rome?
   Why did the ancient Romans throw Christians to the lions?

2. Everyone *was captivated* by the speaker.
   The speaker grabbed everyone's attention and held it to the end.

3. The logo *was reimagined* by the new designer.
   The new designer reimagined the logo.

4. The puppy *was inoculated* before it *was brought* home.
   The vet inoculated the puppy before we brought it home.
   For this one, I've added the "by so-and-so" in order to put that person in as the subject.

5. Susan *was forced* to testify by court order, but she pled the Fifth.
   Susan received a summons that forced her to testify, but she pled the Fifth.

6. Everyone thought the *Titanic was built* to withstand anything.
   Everyone thought the *Titanic* could withstand anything.
   Removing passive voice doesn't always mean rewriting the sentence. Here I've simply changed the verb.

7. Banks in the Old West *were* often *robbed*.
   Banks in the Old West were easy prey for robbers.
   This isn't a great update because I'm still using a BE verb. I could say something like "People often robbed banks in the Old West," but

then the banks aren't the focus of the sentence. Depending on the context, this could be one of those times when passive is the better choice.

8.   He *was presumed* guilty of cheating because he'd never gotten an A on a test before.

   They accused him of cheating because he'd never gotten an A on a test before.

9.   People on both sides of the issue *were stunned* by the vicious attack.

   The vicious attack stunned people on both sides of the issue.

10.   I don't see how she *was fooled* by such an obvious lie.

   How did she not see through such an obvious lie?

   This is also a good example of showing versus telling. The passive sentence tells ("I don't see how"). The new sentence shows by putting us in the speaker's head.

Choose the Correct Word

1.　"That sweater [complements/~~compliments~~] your eyes beautifully."
    Her [~~complement~~/compliment] made me smile.

2.　I need to [flesh out/~~flush out~~] the plot for my new book.
    The police set up a sting in order to [~~flesh out~~/flush out] the suspect.

3.　The [~~amount~~/number] of people at the party was too much for the [amount/~~number~~] of space to hold them.
    Remember, use number *for things you can count, and use* amount *for things you can't. You can count people but not space.*

4.　After the garage sale, I had [fewer/~~less~~] tchotchkes and [~~fewer~~/less] debt.
    Again, fewer *is a count word and* less *is a volume word—you can count tchotchkes but not debt.*

5.　Preserving the [~~historic~~/historical] site turned out to be a [historic/~~historical~~] decision.

6.　What you [~~implied~~/inferred] from my speech is not at all what I [implied/~~inferred~~].
    HINT: The speaker implies. The listener infers.

7.　Please [ensure/~~insure~~] that you fully [~~ensure~~/insure] your belongings.

8.　We don't have much [farther/~~further~~] to go.
    A degree can help you take your career even [~~farther~~/further].

Generally speaking, farther *refers to physical distance and* further *refers to any other type of distance or depth.*

9.   I felt [nauseous/nauseated] after eating too much ice cream.
     Either answer is acceptable. Traditionally, the correct answer would be nauseated, *but these words have become mostly interchangeable in this context.*

10. To do jazz hands, you need to move [~~all~~/both] hands and [all/~~both~~] ten fingers.
     Both *refers to only two.* All *refers to three or more.*

11. There is great camaraderie [among/~~between~~] the members of the group.
     I can't decide [~~among~~/between] the red and the blue.
     Traditionally, between *refers to only two things; however, "there is great camaraderie between the members of the group" would also be correct because, while there are more than two members, the camaraderie is shared between individual members.*

12. He struggled to deal with the [~~enormity~~/magnitude] of his loss.
     While we could be talking about a huge loss (in which case enormity *would work), it's more likely we're talking about the impact of the loss, in which case* magnitude *is correct.*

13. Although he felt [compelled/~~impelled~~] to stay anonymous, his conscience [~~compelled~~/impelled] him to report the crime.
     The implication is that he feels pressured (probably through fear) to hide his identity (fear compels, not impels), and his morality or sense of right and wrong is pushing him to speak up (morality impels us, not compels us).

14. She saw the Statue of Liberty in 1948 when her family [~~emigrated~~/immigrated] to the US.
Remember, people emigrate from somewhere and immigrate to somewhere—it's all in the prepositions!

15. The house [~~lays~~/lies] at the end of the street where they're currently [laying/~~lying~~] new asphalt.
Is the thing that's lying or laying acting upon itself (lie) or being acted upon by someone or something else (lay)? The house is acting upon itself (so to speak) and the asphalt is being acted upon.

16. She motioned to me and said, "[Set/~~Sit~~] those things down and come [~~set~~/sit] with me for a while."
Similar to lie/lay, if someone or something is acting upon itself, use sit. *If they're being acted upon, use* set.

17. She doesn't sit on the [council/~~counsel~~] anymore, but she still [~~councils~~/counsels] the mayor on a regular basis.
The easy trick here? Council is never a verb.

18. The kids ran [~~passed~~/past] us, and on their way they [passed/~~past~~] the food truck that sits just [~~passed~~/past] the library.
Remember, passed is a verb and is only a verb. Past is never a verb.

19. Their [tortuous/~~torturous~~] scheme left us all feeling a [~~tortuous~~/torturous] sense of dread.

20. I can't decide between the cheese soup and garden salad. The [former/~~latter~~] sounds hearty and delicious, but the [~~former~~/latter] is so much healthier.

21. If you'll allow me to [~~advice~~/advise] you, I think you'll find my [advice/~~advise~~] to be very helpful.

Part of speech, once again, is the key here. If you need a verb, it's advise. *Otherwise, use* advice.

22. Let's [cement/~~concrete~~] the plan before we start mixing the [~~cement~~/concrete].
OK, I didn't give you this definition of cement, *so I'm cheating a bit here. But I'm sure you got it right anyway.*

23. I don't feel very [~~good~~/well] today, so it's a [good/~~well~~] thing that I don't have to go to work.
Remember, use well *when talking about health.*

24. The kitchen [reeked/~~wreaked~~] of onions and garlic, which [~~reeked~~/wreaked] havoc on our dinner party.

25. If your curiosity is [~~peaked~~/~~peeked~~/piqued], then [~~peak~~/peek/~~pique~~] through the window and experience the [peak/~~peek~~/~~pique~~] of bad decorating.

26. She was [racked/~~wracked~~] with guilt after she inadvertently [~~racked~~/wracked] the celebration with her outburst.
We don't generally use wrack *in this way, but this is a correct usage. More importantly, if you chose* wracked *with guilt,* you're not wrong. Rack *and* wrack *are often interchangeable.*

27. It's appropriate for you to feel [bad/~~badly~~] over your inappropriate behavior.
To be fair, it would be correct to say, "Ever since I burned my fingertips, they feel badly," but when you're talking about emotions (instead of your sense of touch), always use bad.

28. Ask the manager [who/~~whom~~] has the black vest on if he knows [~~who~~/whom] we should give our coats to.

In "who has the black vest on," who is the subject. In "whom we should give our coats to," whom is the object (we is the subject). That's how you know the difference—who is a subject; whom is an object.

29. Of the two candidates, I can't decide which one is [better/~~best~~] and which is [worse/~~worst~~]. Although, when there were seven candidates, I knew exactly which one I liked [~~less~~/least]. Better/worse/less/more/-er endings *compare only two things.* Best/worst/least/most/-est endings *compare more than two things.*

30. If the rope comes [loose/~~lose~~], you'll [~~loose~~/lose] the wagon.

31. [~~Its~~/It's] not clear if the dog ran away or if it lost [its/~~it's~~] way.

32. Over [~~their~~/there/~~they're~~] is where the Bakers are putting [their/~~there~~/~~they're~~] pool, and [~~their~~/~~there~~/they're] inviting the whole neighborhood once it's ready.

33. I see [~~your~~/you're] finally selling [your/~~you're~~] old beat-up car.

34. [Who's/~~Whose~~] coming with Alan to the surprise party, and [~~who's~~/whose] car are they driving?

35. Red is a better color for me [than/~~then~~] blue, so I'm going to buy this red shirt, [~~than~~/then] return the blue one I bought yesterday.

36. In order to [reign/~~rein~~] effectively, a king must learn to [~~reign~~/rein] in his ego.

37. [~~Beside~~/Besides] not wanting to be at the game, Amber was also annoyed at having to sit [beside/~~besides~~] Gary.

38. Once she'd received the [~~forward~~/foreword], she was ready to push [forward/~~foreword~~] and self-publish her first book. *Yay!*

Practice *Show, Don't Tell*

1. The city is beautiful at night.

   The lights of the city glitter like jewels sparkling against a backdrop of nothingness as the glass and metal buildings reflect the glow and carve shapes out of the blackness.

   Yes, showing often requires a lot more words than telling, but don't worry about that right now. Master showing, then you can work on doing it with brevity.

2. She felt bad about not showing up to the party.

   She lay on her sofa, curled into a ball, and stared at the TV screen. *You're a bad person.* **She tried to focus her thoughts on the fictional** *Friends* **in front of her instead of the actual friends she'd abandoned.**

3. Everyone thought he was unusual.

   Although the people around him tried to be subtle when he talked to himself or sang out loud or danced while he walked down the street, their whispers and side-eye gave them away.

4. It was a cold and wintery day.

   The thermometer tacked to the side of the barn read fourteen degrees Fahrenheit, and globs of wet snow filled the air and clung to everything they plopped onto.

5. Omar waited impatiently for five o'clock to arrive.

   Omar looked around him and sighed. He tapped his fingertips on his desktop and checked his phone—again. He opened his email, scanned through the unopened messages,

then closed it. He darted his eyes from side to side for a few seconds before checking his phone again.

6. Trevor didn't understand the instructions.
    Trevor stared at the piece of paper that looked to be the one-thousandth copy of the one-thousandth copy with its faded and crooked graphics and text that had been translated by an ancient machine into an unrecognizable form of English. He compared piece A7 in his left hand to the graphic on the page. He looked back and forth and back and forth, and his face wrinkled. After a full minute in this pose, he muttered, "What?"

7. They always arrive late.
    Jack and Karina ran from the parking lot to the front door of the theater to find Adrien waiting with their tickets. As they apologized through their panting for being late, Adrien said, "Oh, don't worry, it doesn't start for another half hour. I lied about the start time because, well, I know you."

8. It was the car of his dreams and he wished he could afford it.
    Charlie stood in front of the '65 Mustang convertible with his head cocked to one side and his eyes wide. As he stared at the car he'd coveted since he was nine, his mind raced. "Upgraded V8 engine . . . whitewall tires . . . massive credit card debt . . . classic bumper-to-bumper white stripes against cherry red paint . . . student loans . . ."

9. Amelia tried not to cry when she broke her ankle.
    Amelia bit her lip and looked up at the sky. *Don't cry, don't cry, don't cry.* She looked at her fire-and-rescue run-toward-the-danger girlfriend and smiled through clenched teeth. "It's really not that bad!"

10. There was nothing Carl could do but wait.

Nurses ran in and out of the door while Carl paced. In the few seconds the door took to close each time, he peered down the hallway, trying to get a glimpse of anything that would tell him something. Emergency scenes from *ER* and *Grey's Anatomy* plagued his thoughts, but the trauma room was too far away for its sights and sounds to reach him. He paced and waited. What else could he do?

Practice Point of View

First-Person Example

I'm not a bridezilla. I'm not. I want what I want. I know that. But I swear that I am not a bridezilla. I don't even like that word (a fact that Phillip has learned the hard way!).

We went to three different bakeries to taste cakes, and each visit went something like this: I tasted each option, savored each bite, considered the pros and cons, made notes about each flavor, and graded them on a ten-point scale with ten being outstanding and one being grotesque. None of the options tried received a score lower than four, but none of them received a score higher than seven either.

Phillip, on the other hand, just shoved each sample into his face and spat crumbs in the air as he exclaimed, "Oh yeah, this is so good!" for every single sample! That's not helpful!

And I'm sorry, but not every sample was "so good." In fact, none of them were. They were either too sweet or too dry or too bland or too everything. The missing wow factor really frustrated me as the day went on.

I was fine at the first shop—disappointed, yes, but fine. But by the time we got to the third shop—and these are top-notch, highly rated bakeries, by the way—I was too tired and frustrated to hold back. The final sample received a score of five. *Five.* I had started the day so excited and optimistic and had ended the day so depressed.

I wanted to be comforted, but could Phillip do that for me? No!

"Kat, some of those cakes were really good. You're being too picky."

Too picky? Is there such a thing for one's wedding day? I think not, and I told him so.

Under his breath (but not *that* under his breath), he said—*and I quote!*—"Who knew I'd be marrying a bridezilla?"

"WHAT?!?!"

Third-Person Limited Example

When Phillip and Kat entered the first bakery that morning, Kat's eyes sparkled and she all but danced on her tiptoes. Phillip smiled at her excitement. She had explained the night before all about her points system for evaluating each cake sample, and he chuckled when she pulled out her wedding journal with three pages of hand-drawn cake charts.

Adorable, he'd thought.

Then things didn't go quite as planned. They tasted each sample at the first bakery, all of which Phillip found to be absurdly delicious. But as they tried each sample, Kat steadily lost the sparkle in her eyes, and her mouth turned down ever so slightly at the corners.

When they were done, Phillip reviewed the scores she'd given each sample. They ranged from four to seven. *Dang*, Phillip thought. *That seems overly harsh.*

But he wanted Kat to be happy, so they moved on to the next bakery appointment. Things didn't go better, and Kat's energy waned even more. The beautiful script she'd used at the start of the day for her notes was devolving into scribbles, and her face had a slight tinge of red to it. Phillip cringed a little when she said, "Well, hopefully the last bakery does better."

It was not to be so, and when the final sample of the day had been scored—an unimpressive five—Phillip drove them home in silence.

Back at their apartment, he read through her notes and scores in detail, and he didn't understand where she was coming from.

Wait, the chocolate cake at the second store got a six? A six? That cake rocked my world!

"Kat," he said, trying to be sensitive, "some of those cakes were really good. Do you think maybe you were being a bit harsh? I mean, I don't think any of our guests would be disappointed in any of the cakes we tried today."

"Are you kidding me right now?" Her face had gone crimson. "This is the single most important day of our lives, Phillip. We have the right to expect perfection. It's OK to want perfection, Phillip."

"OK, but is that really reasonable? I mean, who's perfect?"

Kat's response went on for some time, and Phillip finally acquiesced and suggested that she do other tastings without him since he was clearly not up to the task.

As he walked toward the bedroom, he muttered more loudly than he'd intended, "Who knew I'd be marrying a bridezilla?"

From the living room came a single word—loud and clear.

"WHAT?!?!"

Third-Person Omniscient Example

When Phillip and Kat entered the first bakery that morning, Kat's eyes sparkled and she all but danced on her tiptoes. The thought *I'm ready to be wowed* repeated in her mind. Phillip smiled at her excitement. She had explained the night before all about her points system for evaluating each cake sample, and he chuckled when she pulled out her wedding journal with three pages of hand-drawn cake charts.

Adorable, he'd thought.

Then things didn't go quite as planned. They tasted each sample at the first bakery, all of which Phillip found to be absurdly delicious. But as they tried each sample, Kat steadily lost the sparkle in her eyes, and her mouth turned down ever so slightly at the corners. With each bite, she thought things like *Hmm* and *OK* and *Well . . .,* but not one *Wow* or *Yum* among them.

When they were done, Phillip reviewed the scores she'd given each sample. They ranged from four to seven. *Dang,* Phillip thought. *That seems overly harsh.*

But he wanted Kat to be happy, so they moved on to the next bakery appointment. Things didn't go better, and Kat's energy waned even more. The beautiful script she'd used at the start of the day for her notes was devolving into scribbles, and her face had a slight tinge of red to it. Phillip cringed a little when she said, "Well, hopefully the last bakery does better."

It was not to be so, and when they had tasted the final sample, Kat scrawled a five in the chart and, wanting to hide her feelings from Phillip, she stared up at the ceiling and choked back her tears before he drove them home in silence.

Back at their apartment, Phillip read through her notes and scores in detail, and he didn't understand where she was coming from.

Wait, the chocolate cake at the second store got a six? A six? That cake rocked my world!

"Kat," he said, trying to be sensitive, "some of those cakes were really good. Do you think maybe you were being a bit harsh? I mean, I don't think any of our guests would be disappointed in any of the cakes we tried today."

"Are you kidding me right now?" Her face had gone crimson. "This is the single most important day of our lives, Phillip. We have the right to expect perfection. It's OK to want perfection, Phillip."

"OK, but is that really reasonable? I mean, who's perfect?"

"No one's perfect. Of course. And I'm not—wait, do you think I'm being overly demanding? Phillip, this is what these businesses do. It's their job. And I realize that the world isn't going to stop spinning if the cake at my wedding isn't flawless, but don't tell me you make great wedding cake and then serve me something that sticks to the roof of my mouth. You think all that matters is that they're tasty, but there's a lot more to it than that. And I don't know about you, but I'm only planning to do this once, so the cake better be fantastic!"

"Sure, OK, well, I'm clearly not up to the task, so maybe you should take someone else to other tastings."

Kat scowled. "Fine."

As he walked toward the bedroom, he muttered more loudly than he'd intended, "Who knew I'd be marrying a bridezilla?"

Still in the living room, Kat stood, her eyes bulging and heart racing, and shouted, "WHAT?!?!"

Practice Deep POV

Dionne lit a candle and walked into the kitchen. Darkness enveloped the room beyond the candlelight.

"Man, I hate summer storm season."

She shuddered as the wind howled outside. The chains from the swing set in the backyard clanked as they crashed into each other.

Those are gonna be fun to untangle tomorrow.

"Note to self: Sell the swing set. The kids are too old for it now anyway."

Her phone buzzed and she put it on speaker.

"Hello, Mom."

"Why are you whispering? Are you OK? I heard there are power outages there. Do you have power?"

"I'm trying to demonstrate for the eightieth time that it isn't necessary to yell into a cell phone, Mom. And no, I don't have power, but I'm fine. I have plenty of candles to get me through the night."

"Are you sure? Is Carter there to help you? You sound tired."

"No, the kids are with their dad this weekend, which I guess is good timing. No need for them to deal with this hassle."

"Well, you call them if you need them."

"I will, Mom. I better go. I don't want to run down my phone battery."

She ended the call. "Man, I love my mom, but I am so glad she lives three states away."

Practice Replacing Clichés

1. The cops on my favorite show are always *armed to the teeth.*
    The cops on my favorite show always carry a gazillion guns.

2. Look at that baby! She's *cute as a button*!
    Look at that baby! She's adorable!

3. There's no talking to him right now. He's *high as a kite.*
    There's no talking to him until he comes down out of orbit.

4. They were determined to *make the best of a bad situation.*
    They were determined to navigate their way through the muck, focusing on anything positive they could find.

5. Let me *take a shot in the dark* and say . . . you *woke up on the wrong side of the bed* this morning.
    I'm just guessing here, but I'm thinking you aren't having a good day.

6. My grandparents have always been like *two peas in a pod.*
    My grandparents have always been close. In fact, they still hold hands.

7. It doesn't matter which option you choose. It's *six of one, half dozen of the other.*
    It doesn't matter which option you choose. They both kind of suck.

8. C'mon! Don't be so sensitive. I'm just *yanking your chain*!
    C'mon! Don't be so sensitive. I'm just joking around.

9. Look at all this corrosion. These batteries are *older than dirt.*

    Look at all this corrosion. How long have these batteries been in here?

10. Fighting this merger will definitely be an *uphill battle.*

    We're the underdogs in this fight against the merger—it's not going to be easy.

Appendix B

Subordinating and Coordinating Conjunctions

On the following pages is a perhaps not-quite-comprehensive list of subordinating and coordinating conjunctions.

In the simplest sense, a conjunction is a word or series of words that connects separate clauses, phrases, and words.

Coordinating conjunctions connect two or more things that are grammatically equal to one another.[1]

For example:

She picked up *bread, butter,* and *toast.* (**three nouns**)
Softly and *slowly* (**two adverbs**)
He *bought a new car* and *drove it across country.* (**two verb phrases**)

A coordinating conjunction should never be used to connect unequal elements.

For example:

He walked *up the hill, around the fort,* and *waited for me.*

This sentence combines two prepositional phrases and a verb phrase using the coordinating conjunction *and.* This is incorrect, since prepositional phrases and verb phrases are not the same thing. They cannot be combined in this way. To fix it, change it as follows:

He walked up the hill and around the fort and waited for me.

In this sentence, the two prepositional phrases are combined (up the hill **and** around the fort) **and**, separately, the two verbs are combined (walked **and** waited).

There are seven coordinating conjunctions, which can be remembered using the acronym FANBOYS: *for, and, nor, but, or, yet, so.*

Coordinating conjunctions can connect clauses, phrases, and words; however, subordinating conjunctions connect only clauses. And they connect only clauses that are grammatically *unequal* to one another (one clause is subordinate to another).[2]

Another type of conjunction is the correlative conjunction. Examples include *both–and, either–or,* and *neither–nor.* I think of these as a type of coordinating conjunction because they must combine grammatically equal elements.

List of Conjunctions

Coordinating conjunctions are in italics.

after	if only	so that*
albeit	if when	so—as
although	if—then	such that
and	inasmuch as	supposing
as	in order that	supposing that
as far as	just as	that
as if	lest	then
as long as	neither—nor	though
as much as	*nor*	unless
as soon as	not only—but also	until
as though	notwithstanding	what
as well as	now	when
as—as	now since	whenever
because	now that	where
before	now when	whereas
both—and	once	wherever
but	*or*	where there
either—or	otherwise	whether
else	provided	while
even	provided that	whoever
even if	providing	why
even though	rather	without
except	rather than	*yet*
for	since	
if	*so**	

*Note that *so* is a coordinating conjunction, but *so that* is a subordinating conjunction. The main difference is punctuation—coordinating conjunctions are almost always preceded by a comma whereas subordinating conjunctions are usually not:

I was hungry, so I made a pizza.
(coordinating conjunction)

I made a pizza so that I wouldn't be hungry.
(subordinating conjunction)

I made a pizza so I wouldn't be hungry.
(subordinating conjunction—*that* is understood)

Appendix C

A Partial List of Clichés

The phrases on the following pages should be avoided when possible or used in a unique way.

There are 267 items in this list, and that's only *a drop in the bucket* (make that 268).

a baptism by fire
a chip off the old block
a clean slate
a dark and stormy night
a far cry
a loose cannon
a word to the wise
ace in the hole
ace up one's sleeve
add insult to injury
afraid of one's own shadow
against all odds
all fun and games
all walks of life
always darkest before the dawn
an arm and a leg
an axe to grind
armed to the teeth
as old as time
at the end of the day
at this moment in time
avoid like the plague

babe in the woods
back in the saddle
back to the drawing board
bad to the bone
badge of honor
ballpark figure
barking up the wrong tree

beat around the bush
been there, done that
beggars can't be choosers
behind the eight ball
bend over backward
best thing since sliced bread
better late than never
better safe than sorry
between a rock and a hard place
big cheese
big man on campus
birds of a feather flock together
bite the bullet
bitter end
blast from the past
bleeding heart
blessing in disguise
blood is thicker than water
blow your own horn
boys will be boys
bull in a china shop
bury the hatchet
busy as a bee
by hook or by crook

calm before the storm
cat got your tongue
caught in the crossfire
caught red-handed

champing at the bit
  (yes, *champing*, not *chomping*)
checkered past
clear as a bell
come full circle
come hell or high water
cool as a cucumber
count your blessings
cute as a button

devil is in the details
don't count your chickens before they hatch
don't judge a book by its cover
don't look a gift horse in the
  mouth
don't rock the boat
dressed to kill

early bird catches the worm
easier said than done
easy come, easy go
eat your heart out
eat your words
even the playing field
every dog has its day
everything but the kitchen sink
everything happens for a reason
eye for an eye

fair-weather friend
fall on deaf ears
feast or famine
feather in one's cap
few and far between
fifteen minutes of fame
fish out of water
fit the bill
flat as a pancake
follow your heart
for all intents and purposes
for the birds
force of nature
forgive and forget
free as a bird
from time immemorial

get a kick out of
get the lead out
give the devil his due
go the extra mile
go with the flow
good as gold
growing like a weed

hair of the dog
hand over fist
happy as a clam
hear a pin drop
heard it through the grapevine

high as a kite
hold your tongue
hook, line, and sinker
horse of a different color
hot under the collar

icing on the cake
if the shoe fits
in a nutshell
in any way, shape, or form
in the current climate
in the final analysis
in the nick of time
in the same boat
in this day and age
it ain't over till the fat lady sings
it goes without saying
it's a small world

joined at the hip
jump to conclusions
just the ticket
justice is blind

keep a stiff upper lip
keep the home fires burning
keep your fingers crossed
kick the bucket
kid in a candy store
kill two birds with one stone

knock on wood
knock your socks off

labor of love
last but not least
lay down the law
leaps and bounds
leave no stone unturned
let sleeping dogs lie
let the cat out of the bag
lick your wounds
life's a bitch
light at the end of the tunnel
like a broken record
like clockwork
like taking candy from a baby
like there's no tomorrow
lock, stock, and barrel
long arm of the law
look before you leap
look what the cat dragged in
   (yes, *dragged*, not *drug*)
loose cannon
low man on the totem pole
luck of the draw/Irish

make the best of it
man of few words
march of time/history
mass exodus

moment of truth
more than one way to skin a cat

naked as a jaybird
neither here nor there
never a dull moment
nipped in the bud
no accounting for taste
no crying over spilled milk
no guts, no glory
no pain, no gain
no time like the present
now we're cooking with gas

older than dirt
on cloud nine
on pins and needles
on the tip of my tongue
one foot in the grave
open a can of worms
open the floodgates
opposites attract
out of sight, out of mind

par for the course
patience is a virtue
patience of Job
pay the piper
pay through the nose
perfect storm

pillar of the community
plain as the nose on your face
play your cards right
plenty of fish in the sea
pot calling the kettle black
pull a fast one
pure as the driven snow
put the cart before the horse

raining cats and dogs
reinvent the wheel
road to hell is paved with good
   intentions
roll over in the grave

sands of time
sealed with a kiss
see the light
selling like hotcakes
set the record straight
sharp as a tack
shoot for the moon
shot in the dark
sick as a dog
sink or swim
six of one, half dozen of the other
skate on thin ice
sleep like a baby
smooth as a baby's bottom
snug as a bug in a rug

speak of the devil
spill the beans
stick out like a sore thumb
stop and smell the roses
straw that broke the camel's
    back
stubborn as a mule

take one for the team
take the bull by the horns
takes one to know one
the bigger they are, the harder
    they fall
the fact of the matter
the path of least resistance
thick as thieves
think outside the box
third time's the charm
three sheets to the wind
throw in the towel
tip of the iceberg
too good to be true
too hot to handle
tough as nails
trip down memory lane
two peas in a pod

ugly as sin
under the gun
until the cows come home

up the creek without a paddle
uphill battle

wait for the other shoe to drop
water under the bridge
weather the storm
wet behind the ears
what goes around comes
    around
when all's said and done
when it rains, it pours
when push comes to shove
whirlwind tour
whole nine yards
wild goose chase
winds of change
work like a dog
wouldn't touch with a ten-foot
    pole
writing on the wall
wrong side of the bed

yanking your chain
you are what you eat
you can run, but you can't hide
you win some; you lose some

Glossary

active voice: when the subject of the sentence performs the action of the verb.

adjective: a word that modifies (or describes) a noun.

adverb: a word that modifies or intensifies a verb, adjective, or other adverb.

auxiliary verb: otherwise known as a helping verb, used in combination with another verb to form different tenses and voices.

clause: unlike a phrase, a clause includes both a subject and a predicate (verb).

cliché: a word, phrase, or literary device that has been overused to the point of being trite. *see also linguistic cliché and literary cliché*

coaching: the process of helping an author to flesh out the bones of a story during the writing of the first draft or even before writing has begun; not to be confused with *developmental editing*.

comma splice: connecting two or more independent clauses with a comma but no coordinating conjunction: the wind howled, the thunder crashed.

complex sentence: a sentence made up of one independent clause and at least one dependent clause.

compound sentence: a sentence in which two (or more) independent clauses are joined by a coordinating conjunction.

compound-complex sentence: a sentence with at least two independent clauses joined by a coordinating conjunction and at least one dependent clause.

conjunction: a word that joins other words, phrases, and clauses. Most conjunctions are either *coordinating* or *subordinating*.

conjunctive adverb: an adverb that acts as a conjunction in joining two clauses; most common are *however, therefore,* and *accordingly*.

conjunctive phrase: a phrase that acts as a conjunction in joining two clauses; examples are *that is* and *for example*.

content editing: *see line editing*

coordinating conjunction: a connecting word that joins grammatically equal words, phrases, and clauses.

copyediting: the process of reviewing copy for mistakes, inconsistencies, potential misunderstandings, readability, and clarity; copy editors review grammar, style, word usage, spelling, formatting, etc.

count words: words that indicate individual units that can be counted: leaf, pebble, fears.

deep point of view (POV): a style of writing in which the narrator's voice is silenced so that readers experience the story from deep within the POV character's perspective.

deep third: a term used by some to refer to deep POV; those who use this term consider deep third to be an additional type of third-person narration, along with third-person limited, third-person multiple, and third-person omniscient (i.e., they define it as an actual point of view versus a specific style written in third-person limited).

dependent clause: a clause that includes a subordinating conjunction and cannot stand on its own; it does not contain a complete thought.

developmental editing: the process of helping an author fill in gaps and address major issues in plot, character, setting, etc., usually during or immediately after the writing of the first draft; not to be confused with *coaching*.

editor: a professional who reviews copy for issues and mistakes ranging from plot and character problems to inconsistencies to poor constructions to grammar and style errors.

fiction: a made-up story; may be based on actual events, places, or people, but some aspect of the story must be made up. A true story can be fictionalized by adding/changing characters, rearranging the sequence of events, or altering events.

first person: a type of narration in which one of the characters tells the story from their own perspective; characterized by the use of the pronouns *I, me,* and *we.*

grammar: a system, or the study thereof, of how words come together to form sentences; word usage; how words relate to one another within a sentence.

incomplete sentence: a sentence that is missing a subject or a verb, starts with a coordinating conjunction, has a dependent clause without an independent clause, or includes an incomplete thought, among other possible issues.

independent clause: a clause that contains a complete thought and can stand on its own as a complete sentence.

infinitive: the root form of a verb plus the word *to*: to break, to find.

intransitive: a type of verb that does not require an object: he left, she wondered, they worked.

line editing: the process of reviewing a story for readability, inconsistencies, gaps, clarity, verbosity, etc. Line editors ensure the story is complete, understandable, and well written.

linguistic cliché: an overused word or phrase.

literary cliché: overused conventions of plot, character, setting, etc.

narrative: a story; an event told through a particular point of view; storytelling.

narrative nonfiction: a true story: auto/biography, memoir, etc.

nonfiction: any of several types of writing that relay actual events, give instruction, or impart information without any fictional content (other than for illustrative purposes). Examples include biographies, memoirs, reference books, and self-help books.

nonparallelism: when elements that are not grammatically equal are combined with a coordinating conjunction or in other types of lists: they shopped, had lunch, and they went to a movie (two verb phrases and a clause).

nonrestrictive: a word, phrase, or clause that gives information that is nonessential to the sentence in which it appears; removing it would not change the meaning of the sentence or make the sentence difficult to understand.

nonverbal communication: facial expressions, gestures, utterances, tone of voice—vocal and physical cues that communicate feelings without the use of actual language.

object: the thing in the sentence that is being acted upon; the recipient of the action of the verb: Jill bought a dress (*dress* is the object of the verb *bought*); the noun being linked to another word by a preposition: in the house (*house* is the object of the preposition *in*).

participle: a verb that acts as an adjective.

passive voice: when the subject of the sentence is being acted upon by someone or something else versus performing the action themselves: The ball was thrown by Timmy.

past participle: a verb that acts as an adjective and denotes a completed action; most end in -ed.

peripheral character: a character in a story who does not actually take part in it (a background character); a first-person narrator who is only an observer to the story and does not actually take part in it.

perspective: how a character views, experiences, and interprets the world around them based on their past experiences, beliefs, and personality.

point of view: describes the type of narrator telling the story and how that narrator tells it; there are three points of view: *first person, second person,* and *third person.*

predicate: a verb plus any words that modify it. (She wanted to go to town—*wanted* is the verb; *wanted to go to town* is the full predicate.)

preposition: a word that shows the relationship between a noun and another word in the same sentence; the noun is the object of the preposition. The preposition, its object, and any modifiers form a prepositional phrase. (They ate *at the restaurant.*)

prescriptive nonfiction: a nonnarrative style of writing that explains, teaches, or demonstrates something, including self-help, how-to, and other instructional books (like this one!).

present participle: a verb ending in the suffix -ing that acts as an adjective and denotes a continuing action.

pronoun: a word that takes the place of a noun.

proofreading: in publishing, the process of checking a formatted layout for errors before publication; proofreaders look for typos, misspellings, grammar errors, formatting issues, and more.

protagonist: usually the main character in a story; also a type of first-person narrator who tells the story from their own perspective.

relative clause: a subordinate clause introduced by a relative pronoun and acting as an adjective. (The dog *that I adopted* is very sweet.)

relative pronoun: a pronoun that introduces a relative clause; includes *that, which, who* (*whom/whose*), and *what*.

restrictive: a word, phrase, or clause that is essential to the meaning of the sentence in which it appears.

secondary character: a first-person narrator who is not the main character but is an active participant in the story.

second person: a point of view characterized by the use of the pronouns *you* and *your* in which the reader becomes the main character.

sentence: a grammatical structure with a subject and a verb that begins with a capital letter and ends with appropriate punctuation.

show, don't tell: a style of narrative writing in which detailed descriptions that focus on physical characteristics and actions are used instead of simply stating what is happening.

smart quotes: a software setting that causes apostrophes and quotation marks to automatically be curved or slanted, depending on the font.

split infinitive: an infinitive with an adverb or adverbial phrase in the middle: to boldly go.

style: rules governing spelling, capitalization, punctuation, hyphenation, abbreviations, and numbers; rules of written language not covered by grammar.

subject: the word or group of words that are the focus or main point of a sentence; that part of the sentence that is not the predicate. (The store across the street is closed today—*store* is the subject; *the store across the street* is the full subject phrase.)

subordinate clause: *see dependent clause*

subordinating conjunction: a connecting word that joins grammatically unequal clauses.

substantive editing: *see line editing*

tense: the characteristic of a verb that expresses time.

third person: a point of view characterized by the use of the pronouns *he, she, it,* and *they,* without the use of *I, me, we, you,* or *your* in which the story is told by an unknown entity.

third-person limited: a third-person narrator tells the story from a single character's perspective.

third-person multiple: a third-person narrator tells the story from more than one character's perspective.

third-person omniscient: an all-knowing third-person narrator tells the story from any and all characters' perspectives.

transitive: a type of verb that requires an object to complete the meaning of the verb: she held [the door], they bought [a house], he sent [the package] (objects are in brackets).

trope: a literary device (plot, character, setting, etc.) that is easily recognized, is often predictable, and may be considered cliché.

unnamed performer: the person or thing that is performing the action of the verb but is not named in the sentence.

unreliable narrator: a first-person narrator who, for whatever reason, cannot be trusted to be telling the story accurately.

verb: a word that shows an action or state of being.

voice: refers to whether the subject of the sentence is performing the action of the verb (active voice) or is being performed on by someone or something else (passive voice).

volume word: a word that indicates something that cannot be counted in individual units: water, daylight, happiness.

Notes

Chapter 1

1. Thomas Moore Devlin, "The 20 Most Common English Verbs," Babbel, October 3, 2023, https://www.babbel.com/en/magazine/most-common-english-verbs.

2. University of Chicago Press, *The Chicago Manual of Style*, 18th ed. (University of Chicago Press, 2024), 270.

3. *Chicago*, 271.

4. Diana Hacker and Nancy Sommers, *A Writer's Reference*, 9th ed. (Bedford/St. Martin's Macmillan Learning, 2018), 190.

Chapter 4

1. "Singular 'They,'" *Merriam-Webster*, accessed August 17, 2025, https://www.merriam-webster.com/wordsplay/singular-nonbinary-they.

Chapter 5

1. "Rack," *Merriam-Webster*, accessed October 27, 2023, https://www.merriam-webster.com/dictionary/rack.

2. Cindy Blanco, PhD, "Dear Duolingo: Why Do Some Languages Have Gender?" *Duolingo* (blog), updated March 3, 2026, https://blog.duolingo.com/what-is-grammatical-gender/.

3. "Stylebook on LGBTQ+ Terminology," The Association of LGBTQ+ Journalists, Reporting Resources, accessed January 25, 2026, https://www.nlgja.org/stylebook-on-lgbtq-terminology/.

Chapter 7

1. University of Chicago Press, *The Chicago Manual of Style*, 18th ed. (University of Chicago Press, 2024), 392.

2. *Chicago*, 392.

3. These are just examples. *Chicago* doesn't necessarily require commas of this sort when dealing with relationships.

4. *Chicago*, 385.

5. *Chicago*, 429. I actually wrote this line before realizing that CMOS uses almost identical wording. So while this was an original thought, credit to them for saying it first.

6. *Chicago*, 446–447.

7. *Chicago*, 449.

Chapter 8

1. MasterClass, "How to Write a Perfect Paragraph," updated August 23, 2021, https://www.masterclass.com/articles/how-to-write-a-perfect-paragraph.

2. "Literally," *Merriam-Webster*, accessed August 17, 2025, https://www.merriam-webster.com/dictionary/literally.

Chapter 9

1. It's not required to italicize *show, don't tell*. The comma isn't even standard, because there are no standards in the formatting of this term. I've used italics for readability purposes only.

2. Kristen Kieffer, "How to Balance 'Show, Don't Tell' in Your Writing," *Well-Storied* (blog), October 24, 2018, https://www.well-storied.com/blog/what-does-show-dont-tell-really-mean.

Chapter 10

1. "What's the Difference Between Perspective and Point of

View?" *NY Book Editors* (blog), accessed January 22, 2019, https://nybookeditors.com/2016/02/whats-the-difference-between-perspective-and-point-of-view/.

2. Neil Patrick Harris, *Choose Your Own Autobiography* (Crown Archetype, 2014), 1.

3. Ernest Hemingway, *A Farewell to Arms* (Scribner Classic/Collier, 1986), 227–228.

Chapter 11

1. Lori Brown, "Embracing the Mystery: Deep POV," *Writers in the Storm* (blog), January 7, 2022, https://writersinthestormblog.com/2022/01/embracing-the-mystery-deep-pov/.

Chapter 12

1. "681 Clichés to Avoid in Your Creative Writing," *Be a Better Writer* (blog), accessed August 17, 2025, https://www.be-a-better-writer.com/cliches.html.

Appendix B

1. University of Chicago Press, *The Chicago Manual of Style*, 18th ed. (University of Chicago Press, 2024), 300.

2. *Chicago*, 300–301.

Bibliography

"American and British English Spelling Differences." Wikipedia. Accessed March 6, 2019. https://en.wikipedia.org/wiki/American_and_British_English_spelling_differences.

Association of LGBTQ+ Journalists, The. "Stylebook on LGBTQ+ Terminology." Reporting Resources. Accessed January 25, 2026. https://www.nlgja.org/stylebook-on-lgbtq-terminology/.

Bingham, Harry. "Show, Don't Tell." *Jericho Writers* (blog). Accessed January 22, 2019. https://jerichowriters.com/show-dont-tell/.

Blanco, Cindy, PhD. "Dear Duolingo: Why Do Some Languages Have Gender?" *Duolingo* (blog). Updated March 3, 2026. https://blog.duolingo.com/what-is-grammatical-gender/.

"British and American Spelling." Grammar. Lexico. Accessed July 7, 2019. This website is no longer available.

Brits, Leona. "My Golden Rules to 'Show Don't Tell.'" *The Writing Cooperative* (blog). July 27, 2018. https://writingcooperative.com/my-golden-rules-to-show-dont-tell-f4d030eca8c9.

Brown, Lori. "Embracing the Mystery: Deep POV." *Writers in the Storm* (blog). January 7, 2022. https://writersinthestormblog.com/2022/01/embracing-the-mystery-deep-pov/.

Brown, Ross. "3 Simple Steps to Master the Rule of Show, Don't Tell." *Script* (blog). January 30, 2018. https://scriptmag.com/features/three-steps-to-master-rule-show-dont-tell.

Bunting, Joe. "The Secret of Show, Don't Tell." *The Write Practice* (blog). Accessed January 22, 2019. https://thewritepractice. com/show-dont-tell/.

"Clichés." The Writing Center. University of North Carolina at Chapel Hill. Accessed May 6, 2019. https://writingcenter.unc. edu/tips-and-tools/cliches/.

Devlin, Thomas Moore. "The 20 Most Common English Verbs." Babbel. October 3, 2023. https://www.babbel.com/en/ magazine/most-common-english-verbs.

"First-Person Narration." *Literature Glossary* (blog). Shmoop. Accessed March 20, 2019. https://www.shmoop.com/literature- glossary/first-person-narration.html.

"5 Writing Clichés to Avoid." *NY Book Editors* (blog). Accessed May 6, 2019. https://nybookeditors.com/2018/06/5-writing- cliches-to-avoid/.

Fox, John. "The 5 Lessons You Must Know about Cliches in Writing." *Bookfox* (blog). Accessed May 6, 2019. https:// thejohnfox.com/2016/06/avoid-cliches-in-writing/.

Hacker, Diana, and Nancy Sommers. *A Writer's Reference*, 9th ed. Bedford/St. Martin's Macmillan Learning. 2018.

Harris, Neil Patrick. *Choose Your Own Autobiography*. Crown Archetype. 2014.

Hemingway, Ernest. *A Farewell to Arms*. Scribner Classic/Collier, 1986.

Jenkins, Jerry. "Show, Don't Tell: What You Need to Know." *Jerry*

Jenkins (blog). Accessed January 22, 2019. https://jerryjenkins.com/show-dont-tell/.

Kieffer, Kristen. "How to Balance 'Show, Don't Tell' in Your Writing." *Well-storied.* (blog). October 24, 2018. https://www.well-storied.com/blog/what-does-show-dont-tell-really-mean.

MasterClass. "How to Write a Perfect Paragraph." Updated August 23, 2021. https://www.masterclass.com/articles/how-to-write-a-perfect-paragraph.

Merriam-Webster. https://www.merriam-webster.com/.

Selgin, Peter. "10 Tips to Avoid Clichés in Writing." *Writer's Digest*. January 31, 2012. https://www.writersdigest.com/whats-new/10-tips-to-bypass-cliche-and-melodrama.

"Show, Don't Tell: How to Master It (With Examples)." *Reedsy* (blog). May 10, 2018. https://reedsy.com/blog/show-dont-tell/. (modified July 11, 2019, now titled "Show, Don't Tell: Tips and Examples of the Golden Rule").

"681 Clichés to Avoid in Your Creative Writing." *Be a Better Writer* (blog). Accessed May 6, 2019. https://www.be-a-better-writer.com/cliches.html.

"Stylebook on LGBTQ+ Terminology." The Association of LGBTQ+ Journalists. Reporting Resources. Accessed January 25, 2026. https://www.nlgja.org/stylebook-on-lgbtq-terminology/.

University of Chicago Press. *The Chicago Manual of Style*, 18th ed. University of Chicago Press, 2024. https://www.chicagomanualofstyle.org/home.html.

"What is a Cliché? Definition, Examples, and How to Avoid Them." *Now Novel* (blog). Updated June 11, 2025. https://nownovel. com/cliche-examples-avoid-unoriginality/.

"What's the Difference Between Perspective and Point of View?" *NY Book Editors* (blog). Accessed January 22, 2019. https:// nybookeditors.com/2016/02/whats-the-difference-between-perspective-and-point-of-view/.

Wiehardt, Ginny. "What is Second-Person Point of View in Fiction?" *The Balance Careers* (blog). Updated June 18, 2019. This website is no longer available.

Acknowledgments

I thanked a bunch of people in my first edition of this book, but this edition I pretty much did on my own.

Ha! Oh, as if that idea isn't completely absurd!

I owe so much to so many people. Yes, I wrote the book on my own, but I'm inspired every day, mostly by my sister and roomie, Jennifer, who pushes me in directions I don't usually want to go in and who reminded me that the cover should match the tone of the book (so if the cover gives you a chuckle, you know who to thank). And, of course, there's my amazing mom, Chrys, who gave me my creative soul, my voice, and my never-ending desire to tell people what to do. Thanks, Mom!

I also need to thank my writing group—Charlene, Brandy, Kimber, Kim, Bill, and past members who helped with the first edition—for their invaluable input, support, and praise. You lift me up, my friends.

And speaking of friends, I don't know where I would be without my dearest peeps who've been cheering me on for so very many years (that's a lot of intensifiers in a row!): Kelly, Mardra, Marcus, Quinn, Camille (since we were five!), Anne, and Melissa. I love you all!

And to those who are no longer with us but who influenced me so much: My dad, Vern, who, upon hearing I was writing a second edition, would have asked, "Did anyone buy the first book?" He really would have been proud of me though. And Gene, my stepfather, who always cheered and encouraged, all while (purposely) murdering the English language right in front of me.

Finally, my great thanks to two badass women, without whom I would still be strictly amateur at this publishing gig: Ally Machate from The Writer's Ally, who has taught me and continues to teach me so much about writing and publishing (and still working on the marketing!). I was not truly connected to the publishing community until I met you. And Emily Hitchcock, maker of amazing epub files (wink, wink), design guru, and publisher extraordinaire. Thank you, thank you, thank you.

About the Author

Julie Haase is a freelance copy editor and author, the Online Business and Publishing Manager for The Writer's Ally, and the former Publications Chair for the Nebraska Writers Guild. Julie has earned an editing certificate from the University of California Berkeley Extension and enjoys editing both fiction and nonfiction.

Julie has found great satisfaction from teaching authors how to make their writing more effective and engaging for readers. She has taught several workshops at the annual Nebraska Writers Guild conference, which has been one of the many joys of her career.

Julie lives in Omaha, Nebraska, and is a proud mom to her cats, Paul and Ringo.